House Prices
and Inflation

House Prices and Inflation

John A. Tuccillo
and
Kevin E. Villani,
Editors

An Urban Institute Book

 THE URBAN INSTITUTE PRESS · WASHINGTON, D.C.

Acknowledgement. "Inflation and Extraordinary Returns on Owner-Occupied Housing: Some Implications for Capital Allocation and Productivity Growth,"by Patric H. Hendershott and Sheng Cheng Hu is reprinted as chapter two of this volume. It was first published in *The Journal of Macroeconomics,* Volume 3, No. 2 (1981), pages 177-203, and is reproduced here by permission of the copyright owner. Copyright © by The Wayne State University Press.

LC 81-53062
ISBN 87766-306-8

Printed in the United States of America

Please refer to URI 33300 when ordering

A/81

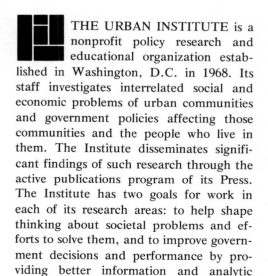 THE URBAN INSTITUTE is a nonprofit policy research and educational organization established in Washington, D.C. in 1968. Its staff investigates interrelated social and economic problems of urban communities and government policies affecting those communities and the people who live in them. The Institute disseminates significant findings of such research through the active publications program of its Press. The Institute has two goals for work in each of its research areas: to help shape thinking about societal problems and efforts to solve them, and to improve government decisions and performance by providing better information and analytic tools.

Through work that ranges from broad conceptual studies to administrative and technical assistance, Institute researchers contribute to the stock of knowledge available to public officials and to private individuals and groups concerned with formulating and implementing more efficient and effective government policy.

Conclusions or opinions expressed are those of the authors and do not necessarily reflect the views of other staff members, officers or trustees of the Institute, or of any organizations which provide financial support to the Institute.

Michael Assay
Federal Reserve System Board of Governors

John Boyd
Northwestern University

Katherine Bradbury
The Brookings Institution

William Brueggman
Southern Methodist University

Robert Buckley
U.S. Department of Housing and Urban Development

Simone Clemhout
Cornell University

Carol Corrado
Federal Reserve System Board of Governors

David Crowe
U.S. Department of Housing and Urban Development

Frank de Leeuw
U.S. Department of Commerce

Lawrence DeMilner
Congressional Budget Office

Douglas B. Diamond, Jr.
North Carolina State University

Ann J. Dougherty
U.S. Department of Housing and Urban Development

John Ermisch
Policy Studies Institute, London

John L. Goodman, Jr.
The Urban Institute

Robert J. Gordon
Northwestern University

Leo Grebler
University of California, Los Angeles

John Greenlees
Bureau of Labor Statistics

Bruce Hamilton
Johns Hopkins University

Patric H. Hendershott
Purdue University

Edward J. Kane
Ohio State University

Jeannie Karstens
General Accounting Office

James R. Kearl
Brigham Young University

James Kau
University of Georgia

Cary Leahey
Office of Management and Budget

Katherine Lyall
Johns Hopkins University

Stephen Malpezzi
The Urban Institute

Neil Mayer
The Urban Institute

Duane McGough
U.S. Department of Housing and Urban Development

Michael Murray
Rand Corporation

Larry Ozanne
The Urban Institute

William H. Reilly
Severna Park, Maryland

Elizabeth Roistacher
Queens College

Michael Schraer
Department of the Environment, London

Robert Schwab
Johns Hopkins University

Lawrence Simons
U.S. Department of Housing and Urban Development

Ann Squire
The Urban Institute

Anthony J. Sulvetta
JRB Associates, Inc.

Craig Swan
University of Minnesota

Thomas Thibodeau
The Urban Institute

Fred Thompson
U.S. Department of Housing and Urban Development

John A. Tuccillo
The Urban Institute

Donald Tucker
U.S. House of Representatives

Robert Van Order
U.S. Department of Housing and Urban Development

Kevin E. Villani
U.S. Department of Housing and Urban Development

Henry C. Wallich
Federal Reserve System Board of Governors

John C. Weicher
The Urban Institute

Steve Weitz
U.S. Department of Housing and Urban Development

Anthony Yezer
George Washington University

CONTENTS

PREFACE

In the past few years federal housing policy has been concerned with two major themes. One is the high cost of homeownership; the other, "the rental housing crisis." Too often, not only the popular discussions of these issues but also proposed policy responses operate in isolation from existing research and analysis. To promote better understanding of these issues, HUD's Office of Policy Development and Research sponsored two conferences that enabled researchers to present and discuss recent important analyses and findings and that provided a forum in which researchers and policy makers could debate the issues.

The first conference was on house prices and was held in March 1980; its proceedings produced the material for the present volume. The second conference, held in November 1980, was on the crisis in rental housing. The proceedings of that conference are being published in a separate volume by The Urban Institute. Readers of this volume on housing prices should find the proceedings of the conference on the decline in rental housing a useful complementary reference.

Both conferences provide fresh insight into the interpretation of past and expected housing market trends and problems. It is the hope of the Office of Policy Development and Research that these two conferences and their proceedings will influence future research as well as policy responses to problems in housing and economic welfare.

HOUSE PRICES
AND INFLATION

1

INTRODUCTION

John A. Tuccillo and Kevin E. Villani

The papers contained in this volume were originally presented at a two-day conference on house prices and inflation sponsored by the Department of Housing and Urban Development and The Urban Institute in April 1980. The first day was devoted to the presentation and discussion of a series of technical papers by a group of about 40 researchers concerned with the impact of inflation on house prices. These papers, with the accompanying formal comments, form chapters 2 through 11 of this volume. The informal comments from the audience are summarized in this introduction.

The second day of the conference focused on the policy implications of the rapid increase of house prices. The program for that day consisted of a panel discussion by five policy analysts and an address by Henry C. Wallich, a member of the Board of Governors of the Federal Reserve System. The proceedings from the second day are reported in chapters 12 and 13 of this book.

The conference stemmed from a growing concern among analysts and policy makers about the heavy investment in housing that had occurred during the middle and late seventies. This phenomenon was (and is) puz-

[John A. Tuccillo is senior research associate, The Urban Institute. Kevin E. Villani is acting deputy assistant secretary for economic affairs, U.S. Department of Housing and Urban Development.]

zling in that the rapid increase in house prices and interest rates increased the cash flow necessary to carry a house but seemingly had little effect on the desire of households to own houses. The late seventies were years of historically high, and in some cases record, home sales. The phenomenon is also potentially serious because excessive investment in housing, which may be the result of the combination of high prices and high demand, could draw funds away from plant and equipment investment and diminish productivity and growth in the long run.

Housing and inflation is clearly a topic which concerns not only the research community but a large number of government agencies and private institutions. Housing accounts for nearly a quarter of the Consumer Price Index (CPI): as housing costs rise, so too do public transfer payments and private wage levels that are linked to the CPI. Thus, while a major purpose of this conference was to enable interested investigators to share their ideas, past research, and future plans, it was also directed to those units of government concerned with policy making in the context of inflation and to private groups concerned with the housing sector.

THE SETTING OF THE PROBLEM

During the seventies, it gradually became apparent to analysts that a significant run-up of housing prices was occurring. Between 1970 and the end of 1979, annual increases in the Consumer Price Index averaged 7.1 percent; in the same time period, the price of the standard quality house grew at an average annual rate of 9.4 percent. Households, however, had perceived this trend early on and proceeded to buy houses in record numbers during the seventies. Partially because of those record home sales, the rate of inflation as measured by the CPI rose into double digits toward the end of the decade.

The Federal Reserve signaled its concern over the rate of inflation, and the role of financial transactions in boosting that rate, by initiating severe credit controls in October 1979 and by following these with more selective controls in March 1980. Since these controls were aimed at the flow of credit to households, they served to focus attention on (among other things) the housebuying activity of the previous years. The impact of the controls was to push interest rates (including mortgage rates) up to a point where long-term borrowing became less attractive, leading to a decline in the demand for housing and a decline in housing activity. From an annual rate of 1.71 million in June 1979, housing starts fell to .82 million in May 1980 and had only rebounded to 1.46 million by January 1981.

Accompanying this inflation in house prices has been a general concern that housing was becoming increasingly unaffordable. By the mid-seventies, the affordability of housing had become a major issue of public policy and of real concern to HUD. Numerous studies identified alarming trends in the traditional measures of housing expenses. But there is a real question as to the definition of affordability. If we assume the traditional rule of thumb that rent ought to be about 25 percent of income and that housing be no more than two and one-half times income, then a declining percentage of households can afford housing. But if we examine that average income for wage earners and the prices paid by new homebuyers, it becomes apparent that traditional rules of thumb are less and less valid. Since no one told the bulk of households that they could no longer afford housing, they purchased housing in record numbers. Housing starts for single-family homes consistently exceeded predictions through the late seventies despite the crisis of affordable housing. In fact, economic forecasters blamed the strength of housing for the failure of their recession forecasts. The continuing and persistent demand for housing clearly required some thought about (1) the impact of inflation on housing and (2) the manner in which we measure housing costs.

The former deals with the manner in which we define housing costs. Simply measuring cash outlays for housing will overstate the true cost of housing. To get at that true cost, two adjustments are necessary. First of all, cash flows need to be adjusted for the impact of taxes. Homeowners actually pay for housing services in after-tax dollars, since housing services consumed in owner-occupied houses are not taxed and mortgage interest payments and property taxes are deductible. A second adjustment is for capital gains, which have been substantial for most homeowners and which effectively escape taxation. When both these adjustments are made, it turns out that the true cost of housing has been declining despite the increasing rate of inflation. This theme runs through the majority of the papers presented in this volume.

Number (2) deals with the manner in which we construct price indexes. If we are in some sense measuring house prices and housing costs in the wrong way, this will introduce errors into the computation of the CPI. During rapid inflation, there is a growing gap between the traditional way of measuring housing costs and the more accurate way of measuring them, because a progressive tax system makes deductions worth more and thus capital gains become more significant in the return to homeownership. When inflation and interest rates rise, then, the CPI overstates the rate of price change because the housing component is overstated. The size of this error is significant since every point of increase in the CPI represents an increase in federal spending of nearly $2 billion and triggers

increases in private contracts of many billions more. Thus, the CPI is simultaneously our chosen measure of inflation and an engine of inflation.

The issues developed—the impact of inflation on housing investment,
affordability, and the adequacy of the CPI—are the topics treated in the
papers presented at the conference. The remainder of this introduction
summarizes the conclusions of the papers and discussions presented and
the general discussion that followed those presentations.

HOUSE PRICES AND INFLATION

The key to explaining the simultaneous occurance of record home sales
and extraordinarily high house prices lies in understanding the interplay
of inflation and the tax treatment of housing. Inflation increases the implicit rents derived by households from their owned houses and generates
large capital gains on those houses. While purely inflation-generated
gains should have little effect on real wealth, the categories in which housing wealth accrues escape taxation. Since inflation also increases marginal
tax rates, inflation-generated increases in nominal income and nominal
capital gains increase both real income and real wealth after taxes. The
Hendershott-Hu paper is concerned with analyzing and measuring the impact of inflation on housing costs within the framework of capital investment. They argue that the interaction of inflation and the tax system
reduces the real after-tax cost of capital to the homeowner and biases investment toward housing. This leads to an increased demand for housing
and raises the required return to corporate equities to attract funds.

The consequent nominal capital gains to housing are considerable and
have grown with inflation for homeowners in all tax brackets. In the
highest case, a taxpayer in the 45 percent tax bracket who financed a
house with a mortgage equal to 90 percent of the original value of the
house would have averaged a capital gain nearly 15 percent above ex ante
expectations over the 1972–1979 period. These gains result from the interaction of inflation, the tax system, and the fixed-rate mortgage. They
also spawn expectation of high real rates of return in the future and thus
increase the demand for housing as an investment. Buckley and Ermisch,
using a similar framework, establish similar results for the United
Kingdom.

The conference participants generally supported the conclusions drawn
by Hendershott and Hu with some qualifications. Diamond points out
that the excesses of the seventies may be setting the scene for a slump in
the eighties. Such would be the case if the government adopts, and is successful with, a strong antiinflation policy. In that case, the expected rates

of return from housing will not materialize and there may be a negative reaction to housing as an investment. This will rechannel investment funds from housing to plant and equipment investment.

Kearl was somewhat more skeptical about the sources of the gains to housing as postulated by Hendershott and Hu. He suggests that it is necessary to distinguish carefully between changes in the relative price of housing that are generated by inflation and those that are generated by real factors. One particular factor here is the changing demographic pro- file of households. Given large numbers of individuals are entering the prime homebuying ages, one would anticipate an increase in the demand for housing as shelter. This point is supported by the evidence presented by Goodman with respect to population shifts and household formation. Despite the decrease in population in many SMSAs, numbers of house- holds are increasing. Thus, demand for housing ought to remain high simply because of demographic change. Kearl also points out that price and return differentials may, in fact, be beneficial in the allocation of cap- ital. Thus, even if inflation disproportionately favors housing, it is not all that certain that this presents a problem.

The work done by Hamilton and Cooke approaches the problem of house prices and inflation in a somewhat different manner. Using age pro- files and housing stocks, they calculate market-clearing rents over a 25-year period. Their conclusion is that there has been a long-run decline in the rental price of housing, on the order of 2.5 percent per year. The problem with this approach, as Swan and Sulvetta both point out, is that it is unclear whether Hamilton and Cooke are measuring the asset price of housing, construction costs, or the price of service flows. Thus, their con- clusions cannot be readily compared to other work, or evaluated within a policy context.

The general discussion centered around the degree to which financial arrangements have conditioned the reaction of the housing sector to infla- tion. The dominant influence here was the impact of fixed-rate assumable mortgages on house prices. In an inflationary economy, where interest rates rise with expectations of inflation, low rate mortgages carry a pre- mium for the homeowner. This premium translates into higher house prices. Thus, fixed-rate mortgages below the current market give an addi- tional boost to house prices and allow them to exceed the increase in gen- eral prices. This is further compounded by the depressing effect on mort- gage rates of federal subsidy programs. In general, the secondary market activities of federal credit agencies have kept mortgage rates below other capital market rates for similar instruments.

On the other hand, if fixed-rate mortgages are not assumable, their existence may retard the growth of house prices. The owner of a home with a low rate mortgage may be reluctant to trade up, despite the potential capital gains involved in such a move, if trading up entails borrowing at a higher rate and sustaining the transactions costs involved in moving. Whether this effect was sufficiently strong to overcome the inflationary effects of fixed-rate mortgage was a matter of some discussion among the conference participants.

There was a general feeling that consumers of housing had shown themselves to be rational despite the contentions of analysts. Recognizing that an age-income pattern existed for most households, homebuyers had opted to acquire as much housing as their credit constraint would allow and thus exploit both the fixed-rate mortgage and the impact of inflation and taxes on the cost of capital in housing. This behavior may have produced some odd housing matches (e.g., the childless couple in the five-bedroom-plus-family-room suburban house), and may have destroyed the traditional housing rules of thumb, but it was (and is) rational and has led to a build-up of household wealth in the form of housing assets.

MEASURING PRICE CHANGES

Besides differentially increasing house prices, inflation also distorts our primary measure of price change, the CPI. The problem occurs because the CPI measures prices on a before-tax, nominal basis and ignores capital gains. These omissions are particularly important in the case of housing, where so much of the impact of inflation occurs because of tax laws and the build-up of capital gains. Since housing costs make up nearly a quarter of the CPI, the index becomes distorted when prices rise rapidly. Dougherty and Van Order attempt a reconstruction of the owner-occupied housing component of the Consumer Price Index by incorporating tax and capital gains effects. Further, they attempt to incorporate inflationary expectations, which, they argue, is the proper method of modeling the reaction of households to the prospect of capital gains. While they employ a variety of measures to proxy expectations, their results are similar in all cases. Essentially, they find that expected inflation does matter and that the holding period of the house is a crucial determinant of the cost of homeownership. From their estimates, it appears that since 1967 about a quarter of the increase in the Consumer Price Index is spurious, i.e., can be accounted for by errors in measurement of the housing component.

Paradoxically, Ozanne finds that the rental component of the CPI is *understated*. As calculated, the rental index reflects both price changes and quality deterioration, two offsetting influences. Furthermore, the index measures different bundles of services in different areas. Ozanne constructs hedonic indexes for rental housing in 39 SMSAs and compares his index with the CPI rent component. The conclusion is that the CPI rent component is biased downward.

Gillingham, Greenlees, and Reece acknowledge the deficiencies pointed out by Dougherty and Van Order and by Ozanne and describe the efforts by the Bureau of Labor Statistics to reform the index. Essentially, they are attempting to purify the CPI housing component by removing all investment aspects from it. This gets at the primary criticisms of the index, but in a manner different from those suggested. Rather than build in capital gains expectations, they would ignore them completely and model only the flow of services from the housing unit. This would place the homeownership component on the same terms as the rental component. Unfortunately, they reject the notion of incorporating tax effects into the index, on the grounds that taxes are not generally in the measurement of prices. In discussion, Van Order pointed out that in fact indirect taxes were implicitly incorporated into the index and that perhaps the tax treatment of a number of expenditure categories ought to be integrated into the index.

DeMilner pointed out the impact (in dollar terms) of changes in the CPI. Based on his research, he estimates that a one-point change in the index accounts for nearly $2 billion of federal expenditures. He has examined the new experimental indexes proposed by BLS and finds that the new indexes would have lowered the CPI by some two to four percentage points. Such a change would have had a dramatic effect on the federal budget. De Leeuw assesses the three approaches to the measurement of housing costs—current prices, user cost of capital, and rental equivalence—and concludes that there is really no perfect index. Rather, each has drawbacks that need to be recognized in using the CPI.

POLICY IMPLICATIONS

On the second day the panel concerned itself with the policy implications of the housing sector's performance in the current inflation. While the focus was primarily on the future, a good deal of attention was given to the relationship of general macroeconomic policy to housing. Grebler discussed the question of whether monetary policy could have been used to defuse the run-up of housing prices that occurred during 1976–1978. After considering a number of arguments, he concludes that it could not. To do so would have required either general contraction that would have initiated a severe recession or selective controls that would have ultimately been unworkable. The actions of the Federal Reserve in October 1979 and March 1980 are an example of the type of measures that would have to be undertaken. Even so, the fluctuations in monetary policy, argues Simons, have reduced the efficiency of the housing sector. Thus, monetary policy has affected housing through its impact on the methods used by builders.

Simons also looks to the future to identify the issues for the eighties. One of the most important of these is the source of credit for homebuying. Recent fluctuations in interest rates have severely endangered the thrift industry. To maintain the viability of the major lending institutions, it will be necessary to alter the nature of the mortgage instrument to make the return to holding mortgages attractive to a deregulated financial industry. In addition to these financial factors, the relative prices of land and energy and the demographic profile of the homebuying public will shape the course of housing in the eighties.

Weicher develops the demographic question a bit with a discussion of who is purchasing houses and who is finding housing less and less affordable. For the most part, unaffordable housing is being purchased by just the groups that have always purchased housing: the young, upwardly mobile household. For older households, the affordability question is moot, since the extraordinary capital gains associated with inflation give them the means to purchase another house. The problem with affordability, to the extent that it exists, is a problem for the poor and for certain minorities. Here, income has not kept pace with home prices and initial wealth is low. For the bulk of households, however, housing remains attractive, especially if one considers actual purchase.

Kane provides a bit of insight into the behavior described by Weicher by considering the after-tax rate of return to housing. Using data drawn from the Survey of Current Finances, Kane suggests that the return to housing has been differentially high and this has shifted household portfolios toward housing and away from financial assets. The problem with this is that housing carries with it a high portfolio risk in the sense that declines in the rate of inflation will reduce the wealth of the household to a disproportionate degree. Moreover, the differentially high return to housing has altered the behavior of households. Normally, the purchase of housing financed through a fixed-rate mortgage constitutes buying an option on the cost of housing services. With differentially high rates of return attracting households, what had been hedging behavior is turning into speculative behavior.

Swan summed up the conclusions about the future that were shared by most of the panel. Essentially, he shares the concern voiced about the possibility of a decline in the relative price of housing. However, this decline ought to be nothing more than that which typically accompanies a recession. Housing will continue to be a relatively attractive investment to the household due to leverage factors, although it may lose a good bit of its current luster.

CONCLUSIONS

Although this introduction is being written a good bit distant in time from the actual presentation of the papers, the situation that the papers addressed has not changed a great deal. Interest rates and inflation rates are still high, investment in housing is still strong (to some minds too strong), and the impacts of inflation on housing are still a matter for public policy discussion and debate. In the time between the conference and this book, the financial services industry has gone through an extremely unpleasant period, and the projections about the thrift industry offered by Simons appear to be accurate. Since the spring of 1980, the real rate of return to housing has fallen as restrictive monetary policy has increased the user cost of capital in housing. This may be the factor perpetuating the sluggish behavior of the housing sector. The point of the whole exercise is that the analyses presented in this volume, valid at their presentation, remain valid today. We commend them to you as an extremely useful guide to the question of housing and inflation.

2

INFLATION AND EXTRAORDINARY RETURNS ON OWNER-OCCUPIED HOUSING: SOME IMPLICATIONS FOR CAPITAL ALLOCATION AND PRODUCTIVITY GROWTH

Patric H. Hendershott and Sheng-Cheng Hu

Over the past decade, the American economy has been plagued by slow productivity growth and high inflation. Real GNP grew at 2½ percent annual rate from 1973–1978 in contrast to 3⅔ percent annual rate for the 1955–1965 and 1965–1973 periods, and annual productivity growth in the nonfarm private sector fell from 2½ percent in 1955–1965 to 1½ percent in 1965–1973 to less than 1 percent in 1973–1978. The average annual rate of increase in the GNP deflator rose steadily during these periods from 2 percent to 4½ percent to nearly 7 percent. Accompanying these phenomena has been a sharp slowdown in the growth in the capital-labor ratio. The "supply-side" economics has therefore emerged in which the need for an increased share of nonresidential capital in GNP is

[The authors are professors of economics, Purdue University.]

[NOTE. Earlier versions of this paper were presented at the Mid-Year Meetings of the American Real Estate and Urban Economic Association, Washington, D.C., May 23, 1979, and circulated as National Bureau of Economic Research (NBER) Working Paper No. 383. The research was supported by the U.S. Department of Housing and Urban Development under grant H-2987.]

11

stressed. Elsewhere, we have considered the impacts of government tax policies on the user costs for various kinds of capital (1980a) and the effectiveness of reductions in the user costs of capital, brought about by liberalization of depreciation policies, expansion in investment tax credits, or a cut in the corporate income tax rate, in stimulating investment in nonresidential capital (1980b). The question in the present paper is how inflation affects the allocation of capital between residential and nonresidential uses.

While inflation may be public enemy number one for a significant portion of Americans, many homeowners have reaped enormous benefits from inflation during the past decade and a half and promise to continue to do so in the future. These benefits take two forms. First, unanticipated inflation raises both the value of the implicit rents flowing from an existing house and the capital gain earned at the time of sale above those anticipated at the time of purchase. The realized real after-tax return on the equity investment in the house will exceed the anticipated real after-tax return to the extent that (1) the house purchase was financed by a mortgage and/or (2) inflation in house values exceeded general inflation. Second, the eventual increase in anticipated inflation lowers the user cost of capital for owner-occupied housing owing to declines in the real after-tax cost of mortgage financing and yields on alternative financial asset investments, and the decrease is larger for households in higher tax brackets. As a result, more housing is purchased and extraordinary returns are earned (the average product on the incremental purchase exceeds the cost of capital). Extraordinary expected returns on owner-occupied housing raise the required return on corporate equity, depress stock prices, and increase the cost of capital for corporate investments. The combination of the decline in the cost of capital for owner-occupied housing and rise in the user cost for corporate plant and equipment has led to overinvestment in housing, productivity losses for the economy, and slowdown in the growth in real wages.

The first two sections of the paper pertain to the calculation of realized real rates of return on homeowner equity. A framework for making the calculations is provided in section 1, and the results are reported and interpreted in section 2. Results are given for overlapping eight-year intervals between 1956 and 1979 for homeowners in the 0.15, 0.3, and 0.45 marginal tax brackets, and calculations are reported for the contributions to the extraordinary real returns earned of a fixed-rate mortgage (relative to both no mortgage and a variable-rate mortgage) and of differences in relative inflation rates. The next section deals with the impact of increased anticipated inflation on the demand for owner-occupied housing and the efficient allocation of resources. Estimates of extraordinary expected real returns on incremental investment in housing are provided in section 4 and the implications of these returns for the stock market are discussed. A summary concludes the paper.

1. The Conceptual Framework

The after-tax rate of return on equity invested in owner-occupied housing is that discount rate which equates the present value of the after-tax net revenues from the house to the initial equity investment. The gross revenues consist of an implicit flow of net rental services over time and a lump sum at the selling date (asset price net of selling costs and the outstanding mortgage on that date). The costs include flows of mortgage and property tax payments, after allowance for their income tax deductibility.[1] Assume that

- Inflation generates increases in net revenues at the quarterly rate p and housing prices at rate q,
- the house, and thus the implicit rent, deteriorate at the quarterly rate d,
- a fraction of the purchase price is financed with a mortgage at rate i,
- the house is expected to be sold after N periods, at which point a percentage realtor's fee will be paid.

The rate of return, e, is then obtained by solving

$$(1 - \alpha)P_k = \sum_{t=1}^{N} \frac{(1 + p - \gamma_s d)^{t-1}R}{(1 + e)^t}$$

$$- \sum_{t=1}^{N} \frac{(1 - \tau_y)\tau_p(1 + q - \gamma_s d)^{t-1}P_k}{(1 + e)^t}$$

$$- \sum_{t=1}^{N} \frac{PAY_t}{(1 + e)^t} + \sum_{t=1}^{N} \frac{\tau_y iL_{t-1}}{(1 + e)^t}$$

$$+ \frac{(1 - \beta)(1 + q - \gamma_s d)^N P_k - L_N}{(1 + e)^N}, \qquad (1.1)$$

where

α is the loan to value ratio,

β is the realtor's fee in percentage terms,

P_k is the purchase price of the house, including land,

γ_s is the ratio of the price of the structure to the total value of the investment,

R is the implicit rent during the first quarter,

τ_p and τ_y are the property tax rate and the marginal income tax rate of the purchaser,

PAY_t is the mortgage payment made, and

L_t is the loan outstanding at the end of period t.

The left-hand side equals the equity investment. The first sum on the right is the present value of the stream of implicit rents, the second sum the present value (negative) of property tax payments (allowing for their tax deductibility), the third the present value of mortgage payments, the fourth the present value of the tax saving from the interest deductions, and the last term the present value of the large sum remaining after the house is sold and the then outstanding mortgage is repaid.

When the mortgage is a standard fixed-rate, fixed-payment mortgage or when the variable rate is expected to remain at the constant value i through period N.

$$PAY_t = PAY = \frac{(1+i)^M i\alpha P_k}{(1+i)^M - 1} \quad \text{and} \quad L_t = \frac{(1+i)^M - (1+i)^t}{(1+i)^M - 1}\alpha P_k,$$

where M equals the original term-to-maturity (in quarters) of the mortgage. Substituting these expressions into (1.1), employing the general finite sum rule, solving for R and dividing by the general price level P, one obtains the real imputed rent as

$$R/P = \left(\frac{e - p + \gamma_s d}{\delta_p}\right)\frac{P_k}{P}\left[1 - \alpha + \frac{(1 - \tau_y)\tau_p\delta_q}{e - q + \gamma_s d}\right.$$

$$+ (1 - \tau_y)\frac{(1+i)^M \alpha i}{(1+i)^M - 1}\left(\frac{1 - (1+e)^{-N}}{e}\right)$$

$$+ \frac{\tau_y \alpha i}{(1+i)^M - 1}\left(\frac{1 - (1+i)^N(1+e)^{-N}}{e - i}\right)$$

$$+ \ \frac{\alpha(1 + i)^M(1 + e)^{-N}}{(1 + i)^M - 1} \ - \ \frac{\alpha(1 + i)^N(1 + e)^{-N}}{(1 + i)^M - 1}$$

$$\left. - (1 - \delta)(1 - \delta_q) \right] \quad (1.2)$$

where

$$\delta_p = 1 - \frac{(1 + p - \gamma_s d)^N}{(1 + e)^N} \quad \text{and} \quad \delta_q = 1 - \frac{(1 + q - \gamma_s d)^N}{(1 + e)^N}$$

When the variables on the right-hand side of equation (1.2) refer to expected, rather than realized, values, the right side is a real user cost-of-capital expression for owner-occupied housing. This rather complicated user cost is the hurdle rate that the real imputed rent from additional housing investment must exceed in order for the investment to be undertaken. In equilibrium, households will have invested in housing up to the point where equation (1.2) holds. The equilibrium real imputed rent, then, can be computed from the depreciation and expected inflation rates, the structure-value ratio, the terms of the mortgage, the property tax rate and realtor's fees, and the homeowner's expected holding period, income tax rate, and required rate of return. To compute realized rates of return over a given N period span for homeowners in a given tax bracket, one simply plugs in the above-calculated R/P for that tax bracket, replaces p and q with ex post values, and solves for e.

The finite holding period, in conjunction with the addition of the realtor's fee and the multiple inflation and financing rates, makes (1.2) a complicated expression. A series of assumptions can transform (1.2) into a more familiar relationship that better illustrates the primary determinants of R/P. If the required after-tax rate of return equals the after-tax mortgage rate itself, the expected housing inflation rates are equal and there are no selling costs, then one obtains

$$R/P = [(1 - \tau_y)i - q + \gamma_s d + (1 - \tau_y)\tau_p]P_K/P. \quad (1.3)$$

The right side of (1.3) is a simple real user cost of capital expression that reflects the current tax treatment of housing (no taxation of implicit rents and the deductibility of property taxes and mortgage interest) and of interest income (taxation at marginal rate). As can be seen, the higher the tax rate, the lower is the cost of capital. Further, insofar as the mortgage rate does not rise by a multiple of increases in expected inflation, the reduction in the cost of capital owing to taxation is greater the higher is the expected inflation rate.

2.   Extraordinary Realized Real Rates of Return

A. THE UNDERLYING DATA

Observed and Expected Inflation   There are three prices in the model: the price of implicit rents, the price of houses, and the price of other goods. For these three series we use, respectively, the rent component of the Consumer Price Index, the residential construction deflator before 1963 and Bureau of Census constant quality (1974) new house price thereafter, and the Consumer Price Index net of the shelter component. All indices are set equal to unity in the fourth quarter of 1964; thus the real imputed rent equals the gross marginal product (R/P_k) in that period. Given the increase in the economic attractiveness of owner-occupied housing in the 1970s, which will be demonstrated below to have been a result of increased inflation, we would expect rents to rise at a slower rate than prices generally and house prices to rise at a more rapid rate.[2] This has indeed been the case. The ratio of the rent index to the general index fell by 16 percent between 1967 and 1978 and the house price ratio rose by 30 percent. However, this does not mean that such divergencies in inflation rates would be expected in the future. On the other hand, if adjustments in the demand for housing are sluggish owing to substantial pecuniary and non-pecuniary transactions costs, then further relative price changes might reasonably be anticipated. Our procedure will be to specify a general expected inflation rate and then consider how expected housing inflation might deviate from it.

Expected rates of inflation are not directly observable,[3] and there is no agreement in the literature regarding how they can be constructed. Our model of expectations is based upon the work of Frenkel (1975), Mussa (1975), and Modigliani and Sutch (1966). In this work, expectations are allowed to contain both extrapolative and regressive elements. That is, the expected general inflation rate (y) is adjusted in response both to recent rates of change in observed general inflation rates and to differences between the long-run normal expected inflation rate and the currently perceived rate $(y_n - \bar{y})$:

$$\Delta y = \sum_{j=0}^{m} a_i \Delta \bar{y}_{t-j} + b(y_n - \bar{y}), \tag{2.1}$$

where the a_i should decline monotonically. With the normal rate being proxied by a distributed lag on past inflation rates,

$$y = \sum_{j=0}^{m} a_j \Delta \bar{y}_{t-j} + \sum_{i=0}^{n} c_i \bar{y}_{t-k}, \tag{2.2}$$

where the c_i decline monotonically and sum to unity and it is expected that n is greater than m. Further substitution yields

$$y = \sum_{i=0}^{n} \phi_i \bar{y}_{t-i}; \qquad \phi_i = a_i - a_{i-1} + c_i; \qquad \Sigma \phi_i = 1 \tag{2.3}$$

Given that a_i is no less than a_{i-1} with the two equal if i is greater than m and that the c_i decline monotonically, it is expected that the rates of adjustment to change in inflation will decline rapidly at first and slowly later.

The next step is specification of an equation in which the rate of adjustment to changes in inflation can be estimated. Accepting Friedman's (1968) interpretation of Fisher's theory, one can assert that an increase in the rate of inflation expected to persist over a given horizon will produce an equal increase in the nominal interest rate of corresponding maturity.[4] In other words, the expected rate of inflation for a given horizon equals the nominal rate of interest for corresponding maturity less a constant. Fama (1975) has presented empirical results which indicate that this hypothesis cannot be rejected for the market for six-month U.S. Treasury bills. Sargent (1973) has shown that this proposition holds theoretically to the extent that the natural rate hypothesis is accepted and expectations are rational. It also holds under restrictive assumptions when expectations are adaptive. We thus posit the following relationship between an interest rate of the appropriate maturity, i_N, and our expression for expected inflation:[5]

$$i_N = d + \Sigma \phi_i \bar{y}_{t-i} + e(CU - \overline{CU}) + \epsilon, \tag{2.4}$$

where the deviation of the capacity utilization rate (FRB manufacturing index) from its mean is included to capture cyclical movements in the real rate of interest. Because the expected holding period is assumed to be 32 quarters, we have calculated an eight-year new-issue Treasury bond yield from the spot rates implied by a new-issue Treasury yield curve. This yield rises from 4 percent in early 1964 to over 10 percent in late 1979.

Equation (2.4) was estimated over the 1964-1 to 1979-4 period. The inflation rate employed for this purpose is the deflator for nonfood business product, net of energy and the impact of price controls for the 1971–1975 period.[6] The ϕ_i were assumed to lie along a third degree polynomial and the length of the lag was extended as long as the adjustment rates remained positive. The sum of the adjustments was constrained to unity by setting the constant, d, equal to 0.024 (subtracting this from i_N prior to estimation). Rates declined rapidly from 0.15 to 0.04 nine quarters back and eventually approached zero after 15 quarters.[7] The weights imply that 50 percent of an increase in actual inflation is built into the eight-year expected rate within a year and 80 percent within two years. Our resultant expected inflation rate fell from 3¼ percent in 1957 to 1¼ percent in 1963 and 1964, rose to 4½ percent in the 1970–1973 period, jumped to 7 percent in mid-1975, fell back to 5½ percent in early 1977 and rose to 7 percent in late 1979.

It seems reasonable to assume that expected housing inflation rates depend on expected general inflation and recent deviations between housing and general inflation. If expectations are being formed over a short period, the deviations might receive a large weight; if the planning horizon is long, however, the deviations might receive little, if any, weight. We specify the expected housing inflation rates as

$$q = y + \theta(\Sigma\phi_i\bar{q}_{-1} - y)$$

$$= (1 - \theta)y + \theta\Sigma\phi_i\bar{q}_{-i} \tag{2.3a}$$

$$p = (1 - \theta)y + \theta\Sigma\phi_i\bar{p}_{-i}. \tag{2.3b}$$

That is, the expected housing inflation rates are weighted averages of expected general inflation and expected commodity-specific inflation. Given our intermediate eight-year time horizon, the weights have been set equal to 0.5. The resultant expected rental inflation rate is quite close to the expected general inflation rate; the latter exceeded the former by over one-half percentage point in only the 1967–1969 and mid-1974–1975 periods. In contrast, expected house and general inflation diverge markedly. The former exceeded the latter by over one percentage point in 1958–1959, while the reverse was true in the entire 1973–1979 period. Moreover, the difference exceeded 2½ percentage points in 1978–1979.

Unanticipated inflation during a period is defined as the difference between the observed inflation rate during the period and the rate expected at the beginning of the period. Unanticipated inflation was negative (up to 3 percentage points) between the late 1950s and late 1960s, i.e., actual inflation over eight-year intervals in the 1952–1968 period exceeded the inflation expected at the start of these periods. Also, unanticipated inflation in rents, house prices, and goods generally were similar. In the 1970s, however, unanticipated inflation was positive and varied by category. Unanticipated general inflation ranged between 1½ and 3 percentage points per annum. Unanticipated inflation in rents was about a percentage point less, while that in house prices was as much as 2½ percentage points more. Actual house price inflation in the 1971–1972 to 1978–79 period exceeded our estimate of that expected in 1971–1972 by 5 full percentage points.

The Mortgage Terms and Required Return on Equity   The required after-tax return on equity, e, for taxpayers in low to medium marginal tax brackets is taken to be the after-tax mortgage rate because taxable bonds and mortgages, the yields on which are quite close, are reasonable alternatives to putting one's own funds into owner-occupied housing. For taxpayers in higher tax brackets, tax-exempt securities offer a superior return. Because the long-term exempt rate has generally equalled 70 percent of the yield on comparable taxable bonds, it is assumed that

$$e = 0.7i \quad \text{for} \quad \tau_y > 0.3$$

$$e = (1 - \tau_y)i \quad \text{for} \quad \tau_y \le 0.3.$$

For marginal tax rates not more than 0.3, the costs of debt and own financing are the same and thus the cost of capital is independent of the method of financing. For low (0.15) and medium (0.3) tax bracket households, the house purchase is assumed to be 75 percent financed with a 25-year, fixed-rate mortgage. The mortgage yield series utilized is the FHA-HUD series for 1955–1964, the Federal Home Loan Bank's (FHLB) effective rate series for the 1965–1972 period, and the FHLB's effective rate on 75 percent, 25-year new home commitments for the 1973–1979 period (*Federal Home Loan Bank Board (FHLBB) Journal,* June 1978).

For households in higher tax brackets, a higher loan-to-value ratio may be optimal. For example, if the mortgage rate were the same for loan-to-value ratios of 0.75 and 0.9, households in high tax brackets would choose the higher loan-to-value ratio and invest the additional funds in tax-exempt securities, the returns on which exceed the after-tax cost of home mortgage credit. However, the home mortgage rate is not the same for loans with different loan-to-value ratios. Recent data collected by the Federal Home Loan Bank Board (FHLBB) suggest that the mortgage rate on a 90 percent loan-to-value mortgage is about 27 basis points greater than that on a 75 percent mortgage (*FHLBB Journal,* June 1978, p. 18).[8] The tax bracket of the homeowner might have to be substantially above

0.3 for the gains from the investment of additional funds in tax-exempts to outweigh the additional cost of the 27 basis points on the first 75 percent of the house purchase.[9]

The mechanics of the calculation of the marginal tax rate above which homeowners would gain by increasing the loan-to-value ratio can be illustrated simply when the inflation rates are equal ($p = q$) and there are no selling costs. In this case the homeowner should minimize the total after-tax financing rate, r

$$r = \alpha(1 - \tau_y)i + (1 - \alpha)0.7i,$$

where the opportunity cost of own funds invested in housing is assumed to be the tax-exempt yield or $0.7i$. The tax rate at which the household is indifferent between a 75 percent mortgage at rate i and a 90 percent mortgage at rate $i + 27$ basis points is obtained by equating the r's for these two alternatives and solving for the marginal tax rate. The result is

$$\tau_y = \frac{0.045i + 0.243}{0.15i + 0.243} .$$

With $i = 9$, marginal tax rate $= 0.41$. Thus high tax bracket borrowers would optimize by choosing the larger loan. Rates of return are calculated for households in the 0.45 tax bracket for two sets of values, i and loan-to-value ratio $= 0.75$, and $i + 27$ basis points and loan-to-value ratio $= 0.90$.

Lastly, annual depreciation and property tax rates are assumed to be 0.014 and 0.018, respectively, and realtor's fees are set at 6 percent of the value of the house.

B. EXCESS NOMINAL AND REAL RETURNS

Households are assumed to invest in housing up to the point that the return on the last dollar invested yields a real implicit rent such that the expected return over the homeowner's holding period equals the required return on that available on alternative investments. Following the procedure described in section 1, equation (1.2) is first solved for R/P, where e is the required after-tax rate of return and p and q are expected inflation rates, and then resolved for the ex post return, $\bar{e}$, based upon the calculated R/P and ex post inflation rates $\bar{p}$ and $\bar{q}$. The extraordinary nominal returns, $\bar{e} - e$, are then computed. These are reported in table 1 for five overlapping eight-year periods beginning in 1956-1.

Three facts are obvious. First, the extraordinary returns earned on owner-occupied housing have been enormous over the past decade and a half. (This contrasts sharply with the dismal experience of the middle

TABLE 1

EXTRAORDINARY NOMINAL RETURNS EARNED ON INVESTMENT
IN OWNER-OCCUPIED HOUSING (%)

	Marginal Tax Rate	1956–63	1960–67	1964–71	1968–75	1972–79
Excess Nominal Returns[a]						
(1)	0.15	−6.36	0.05	9.48	6.98	10.17
(2)	0.30	−6.53	0.05	9.80	7.10	10.54
(3)	9.45[b]	−6.57	0.23	9.88	7.06	10.66
(4)	0.45[c]	−14.49	0.47	17.36	10.50	14.86
Unanticipated Inflation[d]						
(5) General		−0.75	−0.04	2.26	2.68	2.94
(6) Housing		−2.38	0.49	4.56	2.85	5.32

a. $\bar{e} - e$.
b. Loan-to-value ratio = 0.75.
c. Loan-to-value ratio = 0.90.
d. $\bar{y} - y$ (the CPI index, excluding shelter) for the general inflation rate and $\bar{q} - q$ (the GNP deflator for residential construction before 1963 and the constant quality price index thereafter).

1950s.) For a 75 percent debt-financed purchase, the excess returns have ranged from about 7 to 10½ percent per year. In general, housing has earned a 9 percentage point return above that available on investments in financial assets. This is, of course, a direct result of unanticipated housing inflation [see row (6)] and the leveraged investment in the real housing asset. Second, the more leveraged the investment, the greater are the returns from unanticipated inflation. With a 90 percent loan the rate of return is 3½ to 7½ percentage points higher. Third, the excess returns are largely independent of the tax bracket or income level of the investor, given the extent of leverage. Of course, if higher tax bracket investors took advantage of the higher optimum loan-to-value ratio, their returns would have been much greater.

While the data in table 1 demonstrate that since 1964 households earned substantial excess returns on housing relative to those available on financial assets, one might ask whether homeowners were better off in a real sense. This is equivalent to asking whether excess *real* returns were earned on housing, and the question can be answered by subtracting unanticipated general inflation [row (5) in table 1] from the excess nominal returns. This subtraction reveals that the ex post real return on 75 percent debt-financed owner-occupied housing ($\bar{e} - \bar{y}$) has exceeded the expected real return ($e - y$) by 4 to 7 percent per annum over various subintervals of the 1964–1979 period. The real return is nearly doubled for high income investors with greater leverage.

It should be emphasized that these are spendable real gains. Young, growing families have often used the gains to purchase additional housing. Older shrinking families often realize some gains when moving to a smaller unit, and, with the new reverse mortgages, can borrow automatically against the gains. Often households implicitly realize the gains by borrowing (second mortgages or consumer credit) or by reducing their saving out of current income.

C. SOURCES OF DIFFERENCES IN EX POST AND EXPECTED REAL RETURNS

There are two primary sources of differences between ex post and ex ante real returns: unanticipated inflation in conjunction with the existence of mortgage debt and differences in relative unanticipated inflation rates. To see the importance of the latter, consider equation (1.3) when no mortgage is given. Replacing (1 − the tax rate)i with e, solving for e, and subtracting the expected general inflation rate y from both sides, the expected real rate of return on housing equity is

$$e - y = \frac{R}{P_k} - d - (1 - \tau_y)\tau_p + q - y. \tag{2.5}$$

The ex post equivalent is

$$\bar{e} - \bar{y} = \frac{R}{P_k} - d - (1 - \tau_y)\tau_p + \bar{q} - \bar{y}, \tag{2.6}$$

where bars over variables denote ex post values. Subtracting (2.5) from (2.6) and solving

$$\bar{e} - \bar{y} - (e - y) = \bar{q} - q - (\bar{y} - y). \tag{2.6}'$$

Thus, under these conditions, ex post and ex ante real returns on housing equity would vary one-for-one with differences in unanticipated housing and general inflation rates.

To illustrate the importance of mortgage debt, consider equation (1.3) with (1 − the tax rate)i replaced by the average of debt and equity yields. Solving,

$$(1 - \alpha)(e - q) = \frac{R}{P_k} - d - (1 - \tau_y)\tau_p - \alpha[(1 - \tau_y)i - q]. \tag{2.7}$$

The ex post equivalent, assuming a fixed-rate mortgage and equal inflation rates, is

$$(1 - \alpha)(\bar{e} - \bar{q}) = \frac{R}{P_k} - d - (1 - \tau_y)\tau_p - \alpha[(1 - \tau_y)i - \bar{q}]. \quad (2.8)$$

Subtracting (2.7) from (2.8) and solving

$$\bar{e} - \bar{q} - (e - q) = \frac{\alpha}{1 - \alpha}(\bar{q} - q). \quad (2.8)'$$

With no difference in unanticipated inflation rates ($\bar{q} - q = \bar{y} - y$), the ex post real return on equity will deviate from the expected real return by a multiple of unanticipated inflation.

The contribution of relative unanticipated inflation rates and the existence of a mortgage to the excess ex post real returns earned on housing over the overlapping eight-year periods are computed in table 2 for a hypothetical household in the 30 percent tax bracket who obtained a 75 percent mortgage. The total excess real return at the top of the table is the difference between rows (2) and (5) in table 1. Relative unanticipated housing inflation was especially negative in the 1956–1963 period and positive in the 1964–1971 and 1972–1979 periods. However, the effect on the ex post real return was barely a percentage point in the first two of these periods and less than two percentage points in the last. Clearly, it is the leveraged

TABLE 2

SOURCES OF EXTRAORDINARY REALIZED REAL RETURNS

	1956–63	1960–67	1964–71	1968–75	1972–79
Excess Ex Post Real Returns (marginal tax rate = 0.3, loan-to-value ratio = 0.75)[a]	−5.88	0.19	7.54	4.42	7.60
(1) Owing to Relative Inflation[b]	−1.02	0.07	1.06	0.14	1.72
(2) Owing to Mortgage[c]	−4.88	0.12	6.48	4.28	5.88
(3) Reduction in Ex Post Real Return if VRM Existed[d]	0.92	−0.40	1.28	1.48	0.92

a. Table 1, row (2) less row (5).
b. Obtained by setting loan-to-value ratio = 0.0.
c. Excess ex post real return less amount owing to relative inflation.
d. Assumes index rate is new-issue home mortgage rate.

nature of the investment that is the primary source of extraordinary realized real returns (positive or negative) during periods of unanticipated inflation (positive or negative).

D. VARIABLE-RATE MORTGAGES

The existence of a mortgage will not necessarily result in extraordinary
gains when unanticipated inflation rates are positive (and equal). Assume
that the mortgage has a variable rate $\bar{\imath}$. With $\bar{q} - q = \bar{y} - y$, subtraction
of (2.7) from (2.8), after replacing i in (2.8) with $\bar{\imath}$, yields

$$\bar{e} - \bar{y} - (e - y) = -\frac{\alpha}{1 - \alpha}[(1 - \tau_y)(\bar{\imath} - i) - (\bar{y} - y)]. \qquad (2.9)$$

With $\bar{\imath} = i + (\bar{y} - y)/(1 - $ the tax rate), extraordinary real returns would
necessarily be zero. That is, if the index rate of the variable-rate mortgage
moved with a multiple of unanticipated inflation, such that the realized
real after-tax variable rate equalled the initial rate, then the mortgage
would not provide extraordinary returns during periods of unanticipated
inflation. Of course, no known index rate rises this rapidly because (1) interest rates move with expected inflation which tends to adjust gradually
to unanticipated inflation and (2) the movement tends to be one-for-one,
rather than a multiple.[10] If the index rate were to rise by a percentage of
any change in actual inflation, then (2.9) becomes

$$\bar{e} - \bar{y} - (e - y) = [(1 - \phi) + \tau_y\phi]\frac{\alpha}{1 - \alpha}(\bar{y} - y). \qquad (2.9)'$$

As long as that percentage is less than $1/(1 - $ the tax rate) there are still
gains from unanticipated inflation and these gains are positively related to
one's tax bracket; for a given degree of leverage, variable-rate mortgages
(VRMs) are less "costly" for those in higher tax brackets owing to the
deductibility of interest. However, if higher income households have
greater leverage, as suggested by our analysis, then VRMs would be more
costly.

It is sometimes argued that the existence of variable-rate mortgage
would be "unfair" to existing homeowners during periods of unanticipated inflation because mortgage interest payments would rise unexpectedly. A more relevant question is whether an inflation-induced unexpected rise in mortgage interest would raise or lower homeowners' real
wealth. If the unexpected added interest expense is accompanied by
greater unexpected real capital gains, then homeowners would be better

off in the sense that their realized real return on the housing investment would exceed their expected real return. To address this issue, realized real rates of return were calculated on the assumption that VRMs with an index rate equal to that on newly issued fixed-rate mortgages existed. The differences between ex post returns with fixed-rate mortgages and with VRMs are listed in row (3) of table 2. As can be seen, the reduction in return owing to a VRM never exceeded 1½ percentage points in any eight-year period. Further, the sharp increase in home mortgage rates since 1965 would not have offset more than one-third of the excess real return earned in any of the three eight-year periods. Even with VRMs home-owners would have earned substantial excess real returns during these periods of unanticipated inflation.[11]

3. Expected Inflation, the Demand for Owner-Occupied Housing, and Economic Productivity

Housing economists appear to have turned 180 degrees in the past few years in their views regarding the impact of inflation on housing demand. In the early 1970s the impact of inflation on monthly payments (and down payments to a lesser degree) was the focus of attention. Owing to the widespread use of the fixed-payment mortgage, inflation "tilted" real monthly payments upward during the early years of the mortgage, re-sulting in a sharp increase in the ratio of the initial monthly payment to current income. As a consequence, housing was "unaffordable" to those who would have been able to purchase houses or more housing in the ab-sence of the tilt.[12] The graduated-payment mortgage was advocated as a means of reversing this tilt, and the Emergency Home Purchase Assis-tance Act of 1974 was passed in which mortgage credit was to be made available at below-market interest rates when inflationary conditions were having a severely disproportionate negative effect on the housing industry.

In recent years attention has shifted to the impact of inflation on the underlying equilibrium demand for housing.[13] The unaffordability ar-gument pertains to a perceived disequilibrium where inflation-induced financial constraints hold effective housing demand below the equilibrium level. The underlying equilibrium demand for housing is stimulated by in-flation because the real after-tax return from nonhousing investments and the cost of home mortgage credit decline. Recent (1976–1978) levels of single-family housing sales and production and increases in real housing

prices suggest that the positive impact of inflation on the underlying equilibrium demand for housing has outweighed the negative impact created
by financial constraints. This would not be surprising because the financial constraints probably bind only on potential first-time homebuyers
who have not already reaped extraordinary housing capital gains that
would allow large down payments and thus relatively small monthly payments. In contrast, the stimulation to equilibrium demand applies to both
existing homeowners and potential first-time buyers. In this section the
impact of increases in anticipated inflation on the user cost of capital and
thus the equilibrium demand for housing is analyzed.

A. GRAPHICAL ILLUSTRATION

In equilibrium all households will have purchased owner-occupied
housing up to the point that the percentage implicit rental income earned
on the last dollar of housing equals the real user cost of capital as defined
by the right-hand side of equation (1.2) and denoted by c. A decline in the
user cost of capital would lead households to demand additional bed-
rooms, bathrooms, and family rooms until the utility or implicit rents
from these decline to the lower cost of capital (an increase in the relative
price of houses—P_k/P—would, of course cushion the initial decline in c).
The relation between the implicit rents earned by a representative household in the 15 percent tax bracket and the stock of housing occupied is denoted by the schedule labeled R/P in the left panel of figure 1. Given the
current inflation rate q_0, the cost of capital is c_0 and the quantity of hous-

FIGURE 1

THE IMPACT OF AN INCREASE IN INFLATION ON HOUSING DEMAND

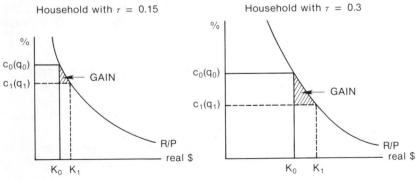

ing demanded is K_0. The R/P schedule and c_0 and K_0 values in the right panel are those relevant to a representative homeowner in the 30 percent tax bracket. The figure is drawn so that the cost of capital is lower for the homeowner in the higher tax bracket. This is true because the net (after-tax) property tax, mortgage interest rate, and opportunity cost of funds are all lower for a homeowner in a higher tax bracket.[14] The importance of the tax bracket to the cost of capital is illustrated most clearly by the simple cost of capital expression on the right side of equation (1.3).

To determine the approximate impact of an increase in expected inflation on the cost of capital, we take the derivative of (1.3) with respect to q. With $P_k/P = 1$,

$$\frac{dc}{dq} = (1 - \tau_y)\frac{\partial i}{\partial q} - 1. \tag{3.1}$$

The cost of capital will decline because the sensitivity of mortgage rates to inflation rates is less than $1/(1 - $ the tax rate), and the decline is greater for households in higher income tax brackets. The impact of an increase in the expected inflation rate and the resultant decline in the user cost on the quantity of housing demanded by the two representative households is indicated by the increases from K_0 to K_1 in figure 1. The extraordinary gains on the incremental investment—the excess of the real rents over the user cost—are indicated by the hatched areas labeled GAIN.

B. USER COSTS OF CAPITAL AND THE EFFICIENT ALLOCATION OF RESOURCES

Real user costs of capital for 32 quarter holding periods are plotted in figure 2 for homebuyers in the 0.15, 0.3, and 0.45 marginal tax brackets. The noteworthy characteristics of the data are expected. First, the user costs or investment hurdle rates are lower the higher the tax bracket. Second, the hurdle rates have declined since 1963 as expected inflation has risen. The decline is especially sharp—6 percentage points—for investors in the 0.45 tax bracket; by late 1978 the user cost is virtually zero.

Given the negligible cost of capital for high-income households, one should not be surprised to find high-income, two-person families owning five-bedroom, three-bath, two-family-room houses. Rapid appreciation rates in house prices and low after-tax mortgage and property tax rates suggest that a larger house should be purchased for investment purposes even if some rooms provide negligible imputed rental income. While the behavior of these households is rational, one might reasonably question whether building these extra rooms is an appropriate use of our national

FIGURE 2

Real User Costs of Capital for Owner-Occupied Housing

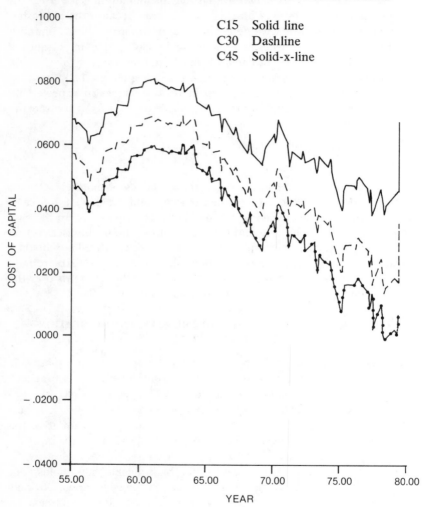

resources. Put in stark terms, is it wise for society to invest in housing earning an annual return of less than 5 percent and forgo investment in corporate plant earning over 20 percent?[15] To the extent that aggregate savings do not increase dollar for dollar with the increase in housing investment, there will be a reduction in the accumulation of business capital and productivity. A recent conservative estimate of the annual productivity loss due overinvestment in owner-occupied housing is 12 billion in 1978 dollars [Hendershott and Hu (1980a)].[16] This loss, which is reflected in lower real wages, is estimated to have more than tripled since the middle 1960s.

A variety of means are available for reducing the tax subsidy to owner-occupied housing. Most obviously, but politically most unlikely, both imputed rents and real capital gains could be taxed. Alternatively, a tax credit could be substituted for the present deduction of interest and property taxes. A tax credit equal to 30 percent of mortgage interest would raise the user cost for those in tax brackets above 30 percent but would also lower the user cost for those in brackets below 30 percent. A 15 percent tax credit would raise the user for all households to that for households in the 15 percent bracket, assuming that all continued to borrow 75 percent of the purchase price. Substantial productivity gains would likely accrue from the latter, although the user cost would still be relatively low for housing. A method for further reallocating the fixed capital stock away from residential capital would be to extend subsidies to business capital, in order to offset those available on owner-occupied housing [Hendershott and Hu (1980a)]. Accelerated depreciation methods (in conjunction with replacement-cost accounting) and investment tax credits are examples. Cessation of the double taxation of corporate dividends and the taxation of nominal gains on corporate equity would also be appropriate. The stimulus to corporate investment would result in a general rise in interest rates and thus a reduction in housing investment.

4. Extraordinary Anticipated Rates of Return, Stock Prices and the Demand for Corporate Capital

Our final task is to compute estimates of the extraordinary gains to households generated by increases in *anticipated* inflation. A rough measure of the gain (the hatched GAIN in figure 1) can be obtained by the approximation

$$\text{GAIN} = \frac{1}{2}(c_0 - c_1)(K_1 - K_0). \tag{4.1}$$

The gain per dollar of additional equity investment is thus

$$\text{GAIN}/[(1 - \alpha)(K_1 - K_0)] = \frac{1}{2(1 - \alpha)} (c_0 - c_1). \tag{4.2}$$

This percentage gain can thus be obtained directly from measures of c at various points in time.

The following scenario underlies the calculations in table 3. Households purchased homes in 1962-4 that provided them with the optimal quantity of housing. A gradual decline in the user cost of capital throughout the remainder of the 1960s caused households to purchase larger houses in 1971-1. These houses were held until 1979-1 when the further fall in the user cost in the 1970s induced the purchase of even larger houses. Table 3 contains estimates of the extraordinary (above that required to induce investment) expected annual real return. The gains are greater in 1979 than in 1971 except for low-income households, are larger for households in higher tax brackets, and largest for households whose optimizing behavior requires them to put only 10 percent down on the incremental purchase.

The expected gains are of sufficient magnitude to have a significant impact on asset prices. For example, if a 3 percentage point increase in the expected rate of return on housing raised the required rate of return on corporate equities from 5 percent to 8 percent, then the value of equity shares would decline by nearly 40 percent. Of course, the extraordinary return is only available on a limited size investment in housing and thus would be expected to have only a temporary effect on share values. However, insofar as expected inflation has continually accelerated and the user cost of owner-occupied housing continually declined, the availability of extraordinary returns has continually reappeared and share values have remained depressed. As a result of the higher cost of equity capital, the user cost of capital for corporate investments has increased and the misallocation of capital toward owner-occupied housing has been further aggravated.

TABLE 3

EXTRAORDINARY EXPECTED REAL RATES OF RETURN (%)

Marginal Tax Rates	Loan-to-Value Ratio	1971–78	1979–86
0.15	0.75	3.52	3.18
0.30	0.75	4.18	5.50
0.45	0.75	4.60	6.66
0.45	0.90	11.40	17.00

5. Summary

Unanticipated inflation results in capital gains that accrue entirely to the homeowner (unless a variable-rate mortgage exists). Thus a homeowner with a leveraged investment earns real, as well as nominal, gains, and these are especially large if housing prices rise more rapidly than prices generally. For houses held for various eight-year intervals between 1964 and 1979 real annual rates of return exceeded expected real returns by 4½ to 8 percentage points. The existence of variable-rate mortgages with an index rate equal to the current mortgage rate would have lowered these excess real returns only slightly to the 3 to 7 percentage point range. Even with VRMs unanticipated inflation benefits homeowners substantially.

Anticipated inflation lowers the user cost of capital for owner-occupied housing, the reduction being greater the higher the tax bracket of the investor, and raises the demand for housing. At late 1978 expected inflation rates, the real user cost of capital, and thus the real implicit rents from owner-occupied housing, for those in high tax brackets is zero. Given that the real user cost of capital for corporate investment in structures is above 20 percent, the favored tax treatment of owner-occupied housing is the source of significant productivity losses for the economy. A variety of tax law changes could be implemented to reduce these losses.

The fall in the cost of capital generated by increased anticipated inflation creates extraordinary expected real returns on incremental investment in housing. This temporarily depresses prices of other assets, most notably corporate equities. Recurring increases in inflation have maintained this depression for a decade and have contributed importantly to the increase in the real user cost for corporate investments. Preventing further acceleration of inflation would allow the value of corporate equities to again reflect the replacement cost of real corporate assets and would reduce the misallocation of real capital.

A final consideration is why, when homeowners gained so enormously from the inflation of the past decade and a half, is there such a concern over the "rising cost of housing"? A plausible answer is the above-mentioned increase in financial constraints that hold effective housing demand below the equilibrium level. The movement to lower percentage down payments and the use of graduated-payment mortgages has, of course, mitigated the impact of these constraints. Regrettably, however, much of the concern about the cost of housing seems to be based upon a misrepresentation of the financial costs of housing: rather than measuring these costs in real after-tax terms, nominal before-tax-costs have been employed. Moreover, this conceptual error has carried over into the computation of the Consumer Price Index, to which many incomes (Social Security, COLAs) are tied.[17] Because the mortgage-interest component, which constitutes 7 percent of the CPI, is the product of a before-tax nominal mortgage rate and a house price series rather than of an after-tax real rate and a price, the component about doubled between the end of 1973 and the first half of 1979. In contrast, a component based upon a real after-tax rate would have fallen sharply, owing to a decline in the real after-tax (marginal tax rate = 0.25) mortgage rate from 3 percent to about $\frac{1}{2}$ percent. The CPI as currently computed rose by 55 percent in this period; with the mortgage-interest cost computed appropriately, the rise would have been only about 40 percent. The annual rate of inflation has been overstated by 2 percentage points throughout the last business cycle.

REFERENCES

Aaron, Henry J. 1972. *Shelter and Subsidies: Who Benefits from Federal Housing Policies?* Brookings Institution.

Diamond, Douglas B., Jr. 1979. "Taxes, Inflation, Speculation, and the Cost of Homeownership: 1963-78." Presented at the Mid-Year Meetings of the American Real Estate and Urban Economic Association. (May 23).

Dougherty, Ann, and Robert Van Order. 1979. "Inflation and Housing Costs." HUD Working Paper.

Fama, Eugene. 1975. "Short-Term Interest Rates as Predictors of Inflation." *American Economic Review.* (June).

Frenkel, Jacob A. 1975. "Inflation and the Formation of Expectations." *Journal of Monetary Economics* 1.

Friedman, Milton. 1968. "The Role of Monetary Policy." *American Economic Review.* (March).

Gordon, Robert J. 1977. "Can the Inflation of the 1970s Be Explained?" *Brookings Papers on Economic Activity* 1.

Hendershott, Patric H. 1979. "The Decline in Share Values: Inflation, Taxation, Profitability and Risk." Presented at a National Bureau of Economic Research Conference on the Taxation of Capital, Cambridge, Massachusetts. (November 17).

————., and Sheng-Cheng Hu. 1980a. "Government-Induced Biases in the Allocation of the Stock of Fixed Capital in the United States." In G. M. von Furstenberg, ed. *Capital Efficiency and Growth.* Ballinger Publishing Co.

————. 1980b. "A Model of Optimal Feasible Replacement Investment: Application to Orders for Producers Equipment." Presented at a Conference on the Economic Effects of Federal Taxes Sponsored by the Brookings Institution, October 1979, and printed as Krannert Institute Paper No. 723. (February). (Forthcoming in Brookings Institution volume.)

––––––., and Kevin E. Villani. 1977. *Regulation and Reform of the Housing Finance System*. American Enterprise Institute for Public Policy.

Laidler, David. 1969. "Income Tax Incentives for Owner-Occupied Housing." In A. C. Harberger and M. J. Bailey, eds. *The Taxation of Income from Capital*. Brookings Institution.

Levi, Maurice D., and John H. Makin. 1978. "Anticipated Inflation and Interest Rates: Further Interpretation of Findings on the Fisher Equation." *American Economic Review*. (December).

Modigliani, Franco, and Richard Sutch. 1966. "Innovations in Interest Rate Policy." *American Economic Review*. (May).

––––––., and Donald Lessard, eds. 1975. *New Mortgage Designs for Stable Housing in an Inflationary Environment*. Federal Reserve Bank of Boston Conference Series, No. 14.

Mussa, Michael. 1975. "Adaptive and Regressive Expectations in a Rationale Model of the Inflationary Process." *Journal of Monetary Economics* 1.

Rosen, Harvey S. 1979. "Housing Decisions and the U.S. Income Tax." *Journal of Public Economics* 11.

Sargent, Thomas J. 1973. "Rational Expectations, The Real Rate of Interest, and the Natural Rate of Unemployment." *Brookings Papers on Economic Activity* 2.

Titman, Sheridan D. 1979. "The Effect of Anticipated Inflation on Housing Market Equilibrium." Working Paper, Carnegie-Mellon University. (March).

Villani, Kevin. 1978. "The Impact of Anticipated and Unanticipated Inflation on House Prices and the Return on Home Ownership." Paper presented at AREUEA Sixth Annual Mid-Year Meeting. (May 23–24).

––––––. 1980. "The Tax Subsidy to Housing in an Inflationary Environment: Implications for After-Tax Housing Costs." In C. F. Sirmans, ed. *Research in Real Estate*. JAI Press, Inc.

White, Michelle, and Larry White. 1977. "The Tax Subsidy to Owner-Occupied Housing: Who Benefits?" *Journal of Public Economics*. (February).

3

Discussions of Patric H. Hendershott and Sheng-Cheng Hu, "Inflation and Extraordinary Returns on Owner-Occupied Housing: Some Implications for Capital Allocation"

Douglas B. Diamond, Jr., first discussant

I must say that Pat has a friend in John Tuccillo. John could have thrown Pat's paper to the eloquent affordability crisis wolves like Ken Rosen or Bernie Frieden. Instead he has sicced on him a more like-minded sheep like myself who agrees with Pat that the user cost of capital and the overall marginal price of housing services has fallen over the seventies, for reasons he so well presented. I think his analysis is well developed and rigorous. I have only a couple of technical comments and one general remark.

My first major comment is that the paper leaves the impression that a drastic decline in the marginal cost of housing has occurred. The analysis emphasizes the decline in the cost of capital. However, at the same time, the cost of residential heating, cooling, and maintenance was rising in real

[The author is assistant professor, North Carolina State University and visiting scholar, U.S. Department of Housing and Urban Development].

terms. Thus the overall cost of housing did not decline as steeply as the cost of capital. However, if the point of the paper is the extent to which capital markets have been distorted, then the neglect of noncapital inputs into housing is appropriate.

I have one other comment about the technical details of the paper. I would like to see them use some more realistic numbers for the required rate of return on equity. They assume that it equals the mortgage interest rate. First of all, your equity in your home is a riskier asset and it is also a less liquid asset, so I think a higher rate of return such as second mortgage rate is appropriate. Second of all, I think that over time and as a result of inflation, the appropriate rate may vary. As real down payments rise and as the real level of mortgage payments rises, I think people are dipping further and further into their sources of credit if they're not debtors and facing higher and higher real costs of debts. I think that one way of looking at the impact of rising real payments in the early years of mortgages during the seventies was that it was raising the cost of capital to individuals by making them go to higher and higher cost sources of credit.

Finally, I would like to spend a little time talking about the implications to be drawn from the paper. Hendershott and Hu suggest that the tax and inflation-induced distortions in the housing market of the seventies have diverted scarce capital resources toward less valuable purposes. Does this mean that new legislative initiatives are needed to balance the distortion?

A case can be made instead for thinking that the 1980s will see an almost automatic correction of the distortion. The case rests on the likelihood that the distortions of the seventies were temporary. In fact some of the decline in the cost of capital for housing was not a distortion to begin with. That portion is due to the decline in before-tax real interest rates. Whether it was due to the accelerating growth in the money stock or a decline in the marginal product of capital due to growth of regulation or energy costs, it is probably temporary. The kind of consistently "tight" monetary policy needed to slow inflation virtually guarantees a return to the before-tax real interest rates of the 1950s (3–4%) or even higher.

Moreover, since reducing inflation is so high on every political agenda, it seems likely that the inflation-induced portion of the decline in homeowner capital costs will also be reversed over time. If this is true and if the real prices of homes themselves stay as high, the real capital cost of owner-occupied housing may quickly move ahead of what it was in 1970. In that case, the policy debate may shift from an efficiency-oriented one to an equity-based concern for first-time homebuyers. And the relative disadvantages to nonhousing investment will disappear.

James R. Kearl, second discussant

Last week I received an editor's rejection of a paper that I had submitted and a referee's comments that noted that the "author's paper satisfied but didn't titillate." He thought that both were requirements for publication; the editor apparently agreed. I supposed that in the language of my referee and in the spirit of that laughter, I think that Pat's paper titillates but doesn't necessarily satisfy.

One of the important insights from macroeconomic research of the past few years is that with inflation there is a serious problem in determining when observed price changes are relative price changes. This problem is particularly acute when there is considerable variability in the inflation rate. Thus, with inflation, it is difficult to distinguish own price changes that are also relative price changes from own price changes that are changes reflecting what "inflation" means. Suppose, however, that relative price changes could be effectively distinguished from price level changes. Then it would be interesting and important to know what part of the relative price change was attributable to or caused by inflation, the overall rise in an aggregate measure of this and other prices. That is, is part of the relative price change a true distortion induced by inflation itself?

Alternatively, one could think of the change in the relative price of housing as having two components: the first part is that change that would have occurred anyway over the past 10 years, say, even if there had been no inflation; the second part is the distortion or change in the relative price attributable to inflation alone. One clearly wants to think of the second part as a distortion and it could be argued (normatively) that it should not have occurred. I don't think that the first part is a distortion nor that we should be very concerned about such changes. Relative prices change all of the time and do so for very good reasons. There were certainly demographic pressures on the housing market over the past 10 years; real income was also rising. Hence, there are probably good reasons to believe that the relative price of housing would have increased if there had been no inflation over the corresponding period and that it should have increased—we should have seen resources moving from other sectors of the economy toward housing construction. A serious problem with Pat's paper, I believe, is that it places everything in the second category—all

[The author is associate professor of economics, Brigham Young University.]

changes in relative prices are attributable to inflation. Pat strongly suggests that somehow we ought to feel uncomfortable with the fact that we are devoting more resources to housing now than we did in the recent past. I don't feel uncomfortable at all about such a reallocation absent serious distortions. I do think that we ought to carefully consider the possibilities of inflation-induced distortions and respond if possible. But if there are strong demographic pressures, say with the postwar baby boom cohort moving into the house-buying and rental markets, we should have seen a change in resource use. Hence, we ought to carefully distinguish changes in resource use that occur because of usual market forces from changes that result from distortions.

It is now common to consider two aspects or components of inflation—anticipated and unanticipated—although the categorization is easier than deciding what really is anticipated and what is not. Again, assuming that such a division can be adequately made, is it really possible for unanticipated inflation to have distorted relative prices and resource use? Pat implies in his paper, or at least I infer from the paper, that it is possible. I think that there are two parts to his argument: first, that unanticipated inflation redistributes wealth because of the use of a fixed interest, long-term, fully amortized mortgage and second, that unanticipated inflation creates uncertainty.

Concerning uncertainty, I think that there is little question that it will in fact distort outcomes. Rick Mishkin and I wrote a paper, published in the *Journal of Finance,* in which we tried to examine the effect of uncertainty on decisions of the sort made in the housing market. We found that households moved toward more liquid assets and out of housing during periods of uncertainty and hence that there was a distortion. However, the effect that we though we observed goes in the opposite direction from that which Pat suggests. There is, however, a problem in linking unanticipated inflation with uncertainty. I suppose that considerable variability in the inflation rate and/or a past history of inflation quite different from that which was expected would create considerable uncertainty about precisely what inflation was going to be. This might be reflected in the notion of unanticipated inflation.

I don't doubt that unanticipated inflation redistributes wealth. However, unless one can make a convincing argument about compositional effects, such a redistribution should not have distorted the price of housing. It might be possible to develop such an argument, but I am skeptical. The argument would have to be developed along one of three lines. For example, one might argue that wealth losses are widely spread across an economy, but that wealth gains are more narrowly focused. Hence there are different elasticities because of the relative size of the redistribution to each individual. One might also argue that the redistribution was from a group not in housing or unable to get into the housing market to a group that could. Finally, one might argue that the redistribution was toward a group with a high propensity to consume housing. The distortion has to be caused by an ex post capital gain. I don't know of any evidence in this area; I don't think that it's in Pat's paper. I do think that one has to be very careful with arguments that involve ex post capital gains or redistributions distorting decisions that are made prior to the redistribution. Essentially, one has to develop an argument that allows one party to anticipate a redistribution while the other party does not or where both anticipate a redistribution, but one party cannot prevent it.

I suppose that I question whether or not we should be concerned with the sort of ex post capital gain problem suggested in the paper, absent some demonstration that it has these compositional effects. These are really rents (I dislike the term "excess returns"). They are rents, and rents always accrue to households when there are fixed stocks and shifts in demand. I could do the same thing that Pat did with housing with IBM or Polaroid stocks for example. If you purchased IBM stock in 1950 you would have done very well; if you purchased the same stock in 1969 you would not have done so well.

Clearly one can find, ex post, winners and calculate the "excess" returns. So what? It is not clear that returns above the "normal" return distorted anything. Indeed, it is not at all clear that from an ex ante perspective there was anything but a normal return. Even if there were such returns above the "normal" return for a short period, they serve the socially useful purpose of moving resources to very productive areas of the economy. But these are ex post rents that are created by shifting demands in an economy. Hence, I doubt you can link comparable rents in housing to the stabilizing argument about inflation that Pat develops and, as a policy matter, one probably should not be concerned about them. They may or may not have income distributional problems, but such rents simply occur in any economy that has stocks and shifts in demand.

Consider next anticipated inflation. Does anticipated inflation change the relative price of housing through distortions of the user cost of capital? Pat's position, and it's one developed in most of the papers thus far, is a partial equilibrium one. That is, if you write out an equation for the user cost of capital treating the taxes in a way consistent with the current tax structure, the partial derivative suggests that there is a distortion from in-

flation that will change the user cost and hence the relative price of housing—a kind of tax subsidy to housing. What does this analysis assume? It
assumes, first, that the real rate of interest is fixed or constant. Next, it
assumes that the nominal rate of interest only changes with the inflation
rate, but not because individuals can win at this tax-subsidy game. Finally, if such an effect on the user cost is to affect the relative price of
housing, it must be assumed that housing is produced at an increasing
cost over some relevant period, both short and long run.

It is kind of a cheap shot generally to say that the analysis is only partial
equilibrium and that someone forgot the general equilibrium impacts
since general equilibrium impacts are very hard to get at and often
speculative. However, I would like to suggest that this analysis suffers
because it is partial equilibrium, and I don't intend such a claim to be a
cheap shot. I really do think that there are some general equilibrium
things that have to be considered. First, one of the implicit assumptions of
Pat's paper and other papers is that the change in the tax treatment
because of inflation changes only the return on housing but does not also
change the return on other assets. But there have been explicit changes in
tax rules in the last 10 years, some perhaps in response to inflation and/or
inflationary distortions elsewhere that have changed the return on alternative assets. In addition, of course, some of the tax distortions with inflation also exist with alternative assets. Hence the appropriate comparison
is the change in the user cost of capital for housing with changes in the
user cost of capital for alternative assets. Some have gone up, some have
gone down. I am not arguing that you can sign the effect one way or the
other. I do think it wrong to implicitly assume that all alternative returns
have been fixed over the past 10 years, and that consequently one can consider the change in the cost of capital in housing alone as an indicator of
what will happen in the housing market. After all, it is relative change
that matters in decisions vis-a-vis alternatives.

Second, Feldstein has argued that the anticipated inflation may, in
fact, change the real rate of interest because of changes in capital inten-
sity, but I don't know where one goes with that argument in the housing
area.

Third, inflation is a tax on money fixed assets. This tax has an impact
on savings, which Boskin and others have considered, and it is conceivable
that savings may increase because of the inflation tax. It certainly has an
impact on the distribution of savings so that individuals will try to avoid
the tax by moving to real assets and out of money fixed assets. Hence, inflation is likely to change the "real" rate of interest in certain assets.

Fourth, and probably most importantly, there is a puzzle in these markets and this analysis. Pat and others have implicitly assumed that the only thing that changes the nominal mortgage interest rate is the anticipated rate of inflation. We are all, in a sense, prisoners of the Fisherian view that the nominal interest rate is the real interest rate plus the anticipated rate of inflation. But in a general equilibrium sense with full adjustment, when there is a progressive tax scheme or other tax distortions, the nominal interest rate should go up by a factor more than the rate of inflation. I don't know that it has happened. It depends a little on what one thinks the real rate of interest is, and what one believes anticipated inflation to be. It appears, however, not to have happened, and that is the puzzle. Why did it not occur? Why are nominal interest rates in general so much lower than one would expect if one properly accounts for the tax savings because of the deduction for nominal interest payments? It appears that households could do very well by moving into leveraged housing—why don't they do so, moving into mortgages, driving up the mortgage interest rate by one over one minus the marginal tax rate, and essentially eliminating the kind of gain with which Pat is concerned? Alternatively, how do we know that the incidence of the tax subsidy is what Pat and others assume it to be? It would seem that those offering to take household mortgages could capture part or all of the subsidy through higher interest rates and that competition for *mortgages* (not housing—the subsidy only appears because homes are not purchased outright) would force precisely this outcome. Hence, the lenders would capture the subsidy, not the borrowers, and there would be little effect on the relative price of housing.

My last comment in this area is that disequilibrium effects have been ignored. Inflation uncertainty may create the liquidity problem that I discussed earlier, where individuals look for more liquid assets and consequently move out of housing. Anticipated inflationary changes in the nominal interest rate, together with the current mortgage contract, tilt the real payment stream. With borrowing rules-of-thumb and difficulties in borrowing against future inflated income, the initial real debt service burden increases substantially when there is inflation and this may make housing less attractive. As suggested earlier, inflation may change the relative price of real and money-fixed assets, inducing a movement into real assets. Essentially, what I am suggesting is that there are good reasons to believe that there are distortions going both ways, hence the net effect of inflation depends on the balance of these effects and is ambiguous. I do not believe that one can sign, a priori, the impact which

Hendershott assumes to exist. Since the impact cannot be signed logically, I think that one can only do what Buckley and Emirsch and others have done—go out and find out what the distortion actually is from appropriate data. I think that the problem is quite clearly an empirical one, not one that can be analyzed by assumption alone.

Finally, it seems to me that Pat is getting at something that is very important. There are compositional effects here that ought to be given serious consideration. Pat considers the compositional effects that occur because of differing tax brackets. Any aggregate study washes all of this. A second compositional effect that seems to be important as well is that inflation has created very different situations, depending upon when a house was purchase. Hence, I applaud the desire to disaggregate in order to understand the dynamics of this market even if I have been somewhat critical of this particular effort.

4

A FINANCIAL MODEL OF HOUSE PRICE BEHAVIOR IN THE UNITED KINGDOM

Robert M. Buckley and John F. Ermisch

Over the past dozen years *real* house prices (i.e., deflated by the personal consumption deflator) in the United Kingdom have exhibited violent fluctuations. Earlier models of the British housing market, which have focused on the consumption aspects of housing choices, have not been very successful in explaining these fluctuations. Our analysis emphasizes the asset portfolio decisions of households, although housing consumption aspects are not ignored.

Models of the U.K. housing market [Artis, Kiernan, and Whitley (1975), Whitehead (1974) (1975), Mayes (1979), and Hadjimatheou (1976)] have five common features: (1) dissatisfaction with stock adjustment models; (2) a focus on the construction of new units; (3) a presumption of a negative relationship between the demand for new housing and the mortgage rates; (4) with the exception of the most recent study, some

[The authors are director, Division of Housing Finance Analysis, U.S. Department of Housing and Urban Development, and research associate, Policy Studies Institute, London, respectively.]

[NOTE: The views expressed in this paper are solely those of the authors and do not necessarily represent opinions of the U.S. Department of Housing and Urban Development or the Policy Studies Institute. The authors would like to thank Patric Hendershott, David Hendry, and Robert Van Order for helpful comments on earlier drafts, and The German Marshall Fund for support.]

difficulty in modeling the impact of Building Society behavior on the demand for housing; and (5) problems with estimating the influence of demographic factors.

The first of these features is not surprising given the nature of the aggregation, and the difficulties and ambiguities inherent in the construction of such a data series. [See Maurice (1968)]. But there is also a theoretical explanation for the estimation problems that have been experienced. If the relative price of housing is not neutral with respect to changes in the anticipated rate of inflation, as is argued below, then measures of the housing stock that use constant prices contain measurement errors which bias the estimates.

The second shared trait, the emphasis on new housing, is also not surprising. Because of the volatility of housing production and its important role in the economy there is a great deal of interest in the factors that influence production levels. Yet although new construction is never more than a small segment of the housing market, there are quite a few participants in this market—builders, government, lenders, savers, new and existing household units, as well as owners of the existing stock of housing. The complexity of the focus has resulted in the construction of fairly elaborate simultaneous equation systems that consider behavior in a small, albeit important, segment of the housing market. And the emphasis has caused less attention to be paid to the behavior of house prices.[1]

The presumption of a negative relationship between the demand for new housing and the mortgage rate may seem to be reasonable in light of similar assumptions in much of traditional monetary theory. However, in this context there are both theoretical and empirical problems with this presumption. As Fair and Jaffee (1972) show, if the U.K. mortgage market is characterized by rationing, then in periods of "excess demand" one may find a positive relationship between the mortgage rate and the demand for housing.[2] Moreover, from a theoretical perspective it is not clear that the presumption is reasonable even in the absence of rationing considerations. Haavelmo has shown that for profit maximizing firms there is no unambiguous relationship between changes in the desired rate of increase in the stock of capital and the interest rate, and Arcelus and Meltzer (1973) have made a similar argument for the demand for housing. Indeed it appears that this view is in fact quite Keynesian in spirit.[3]

Capital assets are capable, in general, of being newly produced. The scale on which they are produced depends, of course, on the relation between their costs of production and the prices they are expected to realize in the market. Thus if the level of the rate of interest taken in conjunction with opinions about their prospective yield raise the price of capital assets, the volume of current investment will be increased.

Of course the behavior of cash-flow constrained households may be very different than that of profit-maximizing firms, particularly in light of the "tilting" of the real payment stream that has been associated with nominal mortgage contracts (see the Department of the Environment [1977] and Kearl [1978, 1979]). Consequently, the presumption may well be very reasonable. But, during periods of high and variable inflation this view implicitly focuses on how the demand for new housing is affected by cash-flow disequilibria rather than utility-maximizing behavior. As Feldstein (1976) has shown, when the return to capital is taxed on a nominal basis, inflation-related increases in interest rates can have a significant impact on the relative yield of tax-favored assets. Given the tax status of owner-occupied housing, it may sometimes be the case that the expected return on owner-occupied housing increases by more than the increase in the cost of capital associated with a higher mortgage rate; at other times the opposite may occur. In any event, because of the tax subsidy the mortgage rate alone does not provide a useful barometer of the effect of credit conditions on housing's equilibrium asset valuation; it only treats the cost side of the decision.

The cost-side focus implicit in existing models is also apparent in specifications that imply that building society behavior has no long-run or an asymmetrical influence on the demand for housing. With the exception of Mayes, interest has only focused on how rationing might have affected housing during periods of credit stringency, assuming that in the long run rationing does not matter. But, if rationing is continuous, then it may also play a role in periods of credit ease. Indeed it seems likely that this view played a part in the establishment of the Joint Advisory Committee on Mortgage Finance in 1973 following the house price increases of the preceding years.

Finally, while the possible importance of demographic factors has been stressed in all previous models, as well as other analyses of the housing market (see Holmans [1970] for example) it is not clear that a satisfactory solution to the data problem has yet been produced. Artis et al. and Mayes ignore the demographic component in their estimation; Hadjimatheou uses (endogenous) marriages, and also follows Whitehead's approach of using a per capita measure of housing demand. The latter approach implicitly assumes a unitary elasticity of demand for housing with respect to population, an assumption that is rejected by the data.

This paper presents a parsimonious model of the housing market that is based on the work of Davidson et al. (1978). It avoids the problem of errors in variables associated with stock adjustment models. The specification is such that short-run disequilibria can be reconciled with long-run theory so that variations in the demand for housing are derived from utility maximizing behavior, and the impact of the rate of inflation on both housing demand and the valuation of the housing stock is explicit. Finally, the paper presents an improved method of dealing with the influence of demographic factors. This method also helps provide insight into the influence of government production of subsidized rental units on the homeownership market.

The paper proceeds as follows: In section 1 a capital asset pricing model of the demand for housing is presented. Section 2 discusses the specification of the model. We then present the empirical results, briefly compare them with those implied by previous analyses, and discuss some of the policy implications.

The Capital Asset Value of Owner-Occupied Housing

An individual household's demand for housing services is generally presumed to be a function of its *permanent* income,[4] the real price of housing services and various demographic characteristics of the household. We therefore can write a typical household's demand for housing services as

$$h_t = h(R_t, Y_{pt}, D_t) \tag{1}$$

where

h = the quantity of housing services

R = the real price of housing services

Y_p = real permanent income; with $h_{yp} > 0$ and $h_R < 0$

D is a vector of demographic characteristics (e.g., ages of household members); and t is a time index.

According to the permanent income hypothesis, consumers process all information available in each period about current and future earnings in assessing their permanent income. In that any information available today about future income is clearly incorporated in today's permanent income, consumers do not *expect* any change in their permanent income. Their assessment of permanent income may, of course, change in the future as a result of unexpected developments, but if they are using the information available efficiently, as the permanent income hypothesis presumes, they expect no change in permanent income. Therefore, by an argument analogous to Hall's (1978), permanent income evolves as a random walk as a result of each consumer's optimization behavior. Hence each household only expects its demand schedule for housing services to change as a result of changes in the elements of D_t. In that the composition of the population in terms of the elements of D_t does not change dramatically over time, the aggregate demand schedule [see figure 1, $Y_{pt}^* = (Y_{pt}^1, Y_{pt}^2, \ldots, Y_{pt}^N)$, where $N =$ the number of households] is also not expected to change over time other than through changes in the number of households.

The stock of housing, H_t, is fixed at any given point in time, and this stock determines the flow of housing services available. We assume that this flow is proportional to the stock, with a constant of proportionality, k. The demand for housing services therefore determines the rental price that clears the market, $\overline{R}_t$ (see figure 1). Clearly, the *expected* value of $\overline{R}$ in the future depends solely on the future size of the housing stock. With given stocks of housing and households consumers can expect $\overline{R}$ to be constant.

The fixed housing stock is also an asset in households' portfolios. In

FIGURE 1

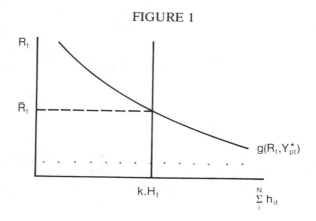

equilibrium, the asset price of housing must satisfy the following relationship in order to induce households to hold that amount of the housing asset:

$$P_H = \overline{R}/C \tag{2}$$

where

$\quad P_H$ is the real price of housing and

$\quad C$ is the real cost of capital for housing purchases.

We ignore for the moment the special financing arrangements available for housing purchases and assume that the (nominal) borrowing rate is equal to the (nominal) opportunity cost of capital in general. The peculiarities of the tax system influence the real cost of capital.

The nominal return on most other assets is taxed, but the return from owner-occupied housing is not taxed. In Britain, neither the imputed rent from owner-occupied housing nor capital gains from it are subject to tax while homeowners, as well as firms, receive tax relief on nominal interest payments. The real after-tax yield from owner-occupied housing may, therefore, increase relative to the yield from other assets with increases in the expected rate of inflation. To get some notion of this effect let us assume that the return from all assets other than owner-occupied housing is subject to tax at the rate of t.[5] Then, C = the expected real, after-tax rate of return from assets other than owner-occupied housing (=the real, after-tax borrowing rate by our earlier assumption); that is

$$c = (r + \pi)(1 - t) - \pi \tag{3}$$

where

$\quad \pi =$ the anticipated rate of inflation, and

$\quad r =$ the real pre-tax rate of return on other assets.

If we assume that the long-run, real pretax rate of return is unaffected by inflation, as American experience suggests,[6] and that asset supplies are fixed, then, from equations (2) and (3),

$$\frac{\partial P_H}{\partial \pi} = \frac{\partial \overline{R}}{\partial \pi}\bigg|c + \frac{\overline{R}t}{c^2} \tag{4}$$

The assumption of fixed asset supplies has implications for tax incidence: the impact of changes in inflation (or tax rates) cannot be shifted. Furthermore, it entails that expected $\overline{R}$ is not affected by inflation from the argument above. Thus,

a function of house prices and income [Ermisch (1980) and Hickman (1974)], as well as subject to considerable measurement error. More precisely, our measure of household formation purely attributable to demographic change is the change in the number of households which would have occurred if the age/sex/marital status-specific household headship rates and marriage proportions observed in 1971 prevailed throughout the estimation period while the age/sex distribution changed as it actually did. The annual changes are interpolated over quarters and then smoothed by a 10-quarter moving average of "net household formation attributable to demographic change" (HH).

The impact of a given number of households on the demand for housing services *in the owner-occupied sector* is conditioned by the stock of housing in the other two main sectors. In particular, since 30 percent of the housing stock is made up of government-owned, subsidized rental units we must also consider the influence of changes in the cost and availability of subsidized (council) housing on the demand for owner-occupied housing. One might expect, as do Artis et al., that lower real council rents would reduce the demand for owner-occupied housing, but this view fails to recognize that because council rents are below market rents, council house tenants as well as those persons on the waiting list are not operating on the margin. Lower real rents may just lengthen the queues for local authority accommodation while these households continue to operate in the private housing market. With this continual excess demand for council housing, change in the supply of council housing is more likely to affect the demand for owner-occupied housing than council rents. We therefore include council house completions (CH) in our specification. Furthermore, we consider the spill-over effect on the demand for owner-occupied housing of previous imbalance between net household formation attributable to demographic change (HH) and the council house production (CH). This is denoted as the "renter flow correction process," which is fully specified in the following section.

Econometric Specification

We start from a specification of the model in equilibrium, and from there derive the disequilibrium specification which is used in the estimation of the parameters of the equilibrium model. If figure 1 is now interpreted as the owner-occupied housing market, it is clear from it that, in reduced form, the real (imputed) rental price of housing services in the owner-occupied sector, R_t^o, can be expressed as a function of average household permanent income, the owner-occupied housing stock (H_t), and the number of households in the economy (the dimension of the vector Y_p^*). What is not so clear from figure 1 (since the earlier discussion focused on fixed stocks) is that the stock of rental housing is also a determinant of the real rental price R^o. It appears that the difference between the number of households and size of the rental stock can summarize the two latter factors, and we denote Q as this difference. In addition to the number of households, however, the size of the increment to the stock of households may directly affect rental levels. It is conceivable that more rapid growth in the number of households may put upward pressure on rents by increasing activity in housing markets. It is therefore hypothesized that a greater volume of net household formation due to demographic changes (HH) raises the real rental price of housing services. Our equilibrium reduced form is then

$$R^o = f(\bar{y}_{pt}, H_t, Q_t, HH_t) \tag{6}$$

where $\bar{y}_{pt}$ is average household permanent income.

Quarterly increments to the stocks of owner-occupied housing, other assets, and households are small in relation to the stocks. Furthermore, the effect of increments to the housing stock on real rents (R^o) are to some extent offset by the effect of additional households relative to the rental stock (i.e., higher Q) on R^o (both H and Q were increasing over our sample period, 1967–1978). Our lack of reliable information on quarterly changes in the owner-occupied housing stock and the number of households less the rental stock is therefore probably not critical for our estimation of the asset demand function for owner-occupied housing. We shall assume that the ratio of the owner-occupied housing stock to the number of households less the rental stock changes randomly over our observation period:

$$\ln(H_t/Q_t) = a + e_t \tag{7}$$

where $E(e) = 0$ and ln is the natural logarithm.

The assumptions encapsulized in equation (7) are obviously designed to justify applying results obtained above in a fixed stock world to the real world. An examination of the available information on the owner-occupied housing stock in terms of units and the number of households less the number of rental units over one sample period suggests that H_t/Q_t has indeed varied very litle. Using these measures of H_t and Q_t, the coefficient of variation of H_t/Q_t was .0085, and there was no indication of an exponential trend (i.e., $E(e) = 0$).

We assume the following functional form for equation (6):

$$\ln R_t^o = \alpha_1 \ln \overline{Y}_{pt} + \alpha_2 \ln (H_t/Q_t) + \alpha_3 \ln HH_t + A \tag{8}$$

As noted earlier, $\overline{Y}_{pt}$ follows a random walk[12]

$$\ln \overline{Y}_{pt} = \ln \overline{Y}_{pt-1} + v_t \tag{9}$$

where $E(v_t) = 0$.

Substituting from (7) into (8):

$$\ln R_t^o = \alpha_1 \ln \overline{Y}_{pt} + \alpha_2(a + {}_{et}) + \alpha_3 \ln HH_t + A \tag{10}$$

and

$$\ln R_{t-1}^o = \alpha_1 \ln \overline{Y}_{pt-1} + \alpha_2(a + {}_{e(t-1)}) + \alpha_3 \ln HH_{t-1} + A \tag{11}$$

Substituting from (9) into (10),

$$\ln R_t^o = \alpha_1 \ln Y_{pt-1} + \alpha_1 v_t + \alpha_2(a + {}_{et}) + \alpha_3 \ln HH_t + A \tag{12}$$

From (11) and (12),

$$E(\Delta \ln R_t^o) = \alpha_3(\Delta \ln HH_t) \tag{13}$$

where $\Delta \ln X_t = \ln X_t - \ln X_{t-1}$ for all X_t

It is clear from (13) that the expected level of the real (imputed) rental price of owner-occupied housing only changes with net household formation attributable to demographic change. So we could equivalently express,

$$\ln R_t^o = \delta_0 + \delta_1 \ln HH_t + U_t \tag{14}$$

where $E(U_t) = 0$, δ_0, $\delta_1 > 0$ (defined for $HH_t > 0$)

From equation (2),

$$\ln P_H = \ln R_t^o - \ln C_t \tag{15}$$

The arguments in the preceding section indicate that the home purchaser's cost of capital is inversely related to the anticipated rate of inflation and the personal tax rate, as captured in S, and to the proportion of personal savings captured by building societies weighted by the mean loan-to-value ratio. We do not include the mortgage rate in our function determining the cost of capital, since we wish to define an equilibrium situation, albeit a short-run one in the sense that the housing stock has had time to adjust. In this equilibrium we presume that building societies have set their mortgage rate so as to achieve their desired gap between their rate and the market rate. If they have done so, then the nominal interest rate less the gap determines the mortgage rate, and RM would, therefore, be redundant if S is included in the cost of capital function. Using a log-linear form for the cost of capital function, C_t, equation (15) implies that we can write the *short-run* equilibrium price of housing (or the demand function for owner-occupied housing) as

$$\ln P_H = \gamma_0' + \gamma_1' \ln HH + \gamma_2' \ln S + \gamma_3' \ln BS + u_t \qquad (16)$$

where

$$\gamma_1' > 0 \qquad i = 0, 1, 2, 3$$
$$\gamma_1' = \delta_1$$

By focusing on permanent income as the prime determinant of the position of a household's housing demand schedule, we have implicitly assumed that the household is not constrained by liquidity considerations. If the household's choices are subject to liquidity constraints, then current disposable income may also influence housing demand. We test for this below by including the log of real, disposable income in equation (16) above.

At first sight this may appear to be a somewhat strange demand function for housing, but when one allows for the likelihood, according to our arguments, that permanent income ($\overline{Y}_p$) and the real interest rate (r) are virtually constant over time this is a theoretically reasonable specification.

We are not, of course, observing a market in equilibrium in each quarter. In particular, household asset portfolios are unlikely to be adjusted completely to changes in the cost of capital for housing. We postulate a particular form of a rational distributed lag model suggested by Davidson et al. This dynamic adjustment model may be viewed as an "error correction" process whereby households react to the disequilibrium situation existing at the beginning of the period. It has the property that equation (16) is satisfied in equilibrium but not at each point in time. So only the *model,* and not the *data,* is forced to satisfy equation (16).

As noted earlier, mortgage rate changes affect housing demand outside of equilibrium, and it is also likely that unanticipated changes in disposable income and government policy affect the demand for housing. Proponents of the permanent income hypothesis suggest that transitory income changes primarily affect savings, and we hypothesize that these changes in savings may take the form of changing one's holdings of housing assets. Changes in home improvement grants from the government would also tend to find a similar outlet. We therefore include changes in real disposable income and home improvement grants in the disequilibrium specification of our model. Finally, as explained earlier, we specify a renter flow correction process to capture the spillover of previous imbalance between demographically induced net household formation and additions to the subsidized rental stock into the demand for housing for owner-occupation. Our dynamic equation (after experimentation) is

$$\Delta \ln P_{Ht} = \beta_1 \Delta \ln S_{t-1} + \beta_2 \Delta \ln BS_{t-2} + \beta_3 \Delta \ln Rm_{t-2}$$

$$+ \beta_4 \Delta \ln Y_t + \beta_5 \Delta \ln Y_{t-1} + \beta_6 \Delta \ln CH_t$$

$$+ \beta_7 \Delta \ln HH_t + \beta_8 \Delta \ln G_t + \gamma_1 \ln HH_{t-1}$$

$$+ \gamma_2 \ln(S_{t-1}/PH_{t-1}) + \gamma_3 \ln(BS_{t-3}/PH_{t-1})$$

$$+ \gamma_4 \ln(HH/CH)_{t-1} + \gamma_0 + e_t \qquad (17)$$

where $\Delta \ln Y_t = \ln Y_t - \ln Y_{t-1}$ and e_t is white noise.

In a steady-state equilibrium $\Delta \ln X_t = 0$ for all X_t, and equation (17) reduces to

$$\ln P_H = \frac{\gamma_0 + \gamma_1 \ln HH}{\gamma_2 + \gamma_3} + \frac{\gamma_2}{\gamma_2 + \gamma_3} \ln S + \frac{\gamma_3 \ln BS}{\gamma_2 + \gamma_3} \qquad (18)$$

which is equilibrium equation (16).

When we included the log of last period's real income in equation (17) and estimated it, its coefficient was not significantly different from zero, so we can reject the inclusion of the log of current real income in equation (16), thus suggesting that liquidiy constraints are not a significant influence on short-run *equilibrium* house prices. Our results, however, suggest that the relaxation/contraction of liquidity constraints may have a disequilibrium influence, although this could, of course, merely reflect the influence of changes in transitory income.

We therefore proceed to estimate equation (17) without using lagged real income, although we shall also consider whether local authority rent levels influence the demand for owner-occupied housing. As noted at the close of the preceding section, we hypothesize that they do not.

Empirical Results

The data employed in estimating the parameters of equation (17) are described fully in the Appendix, but the measure of the dependent variable, real house price, deserves some discussion. It is based upon the average price of dwellings mortgaged with building societies. While building societies provide about 80 percent of mortgages they generally do not deal with the upper and lower ends of the market. It is conceivable that with changes in credit conditions (e.g., changes in BS) the proportion of transactions financed by building societies and the price composition of their loans may alter. This may make the error term, e_t, correlated with some of the regressors (e.b., BS). We do not know if this occurs, nor can we do anything about it, but if it does, then the consistency of our parameter estimates will be damaged.

We have estimated over the period 1967:2 to 1978:2, and the results are shown in table 1. Row (a) was estimated using ordinary least squares (OLS). Given the possibility that S_{t-1}, BS_{t-2}, Rm_{t-2} and Y_t may be endogenous variables, instrumental variables (IV) were used in the other two rows.[13] The signs of all the coefficients are in accord with our hypotheses, and all but one are significant at the 10 percent level.

The coefficients in rows (a) and (b) are with few exceptions very similar, suggesting that simultaneous equations bias may be a consideration in row (a), but not a major concern. For the most part, the coefficients of the potentially endogenous variables increased in absolute value (and relative to their standard errors) when IV was used rather than OLS.

In none of the equations can we strongly reject the hypothesis that the initial impact of anticipated inflation on the relative price of housing is less than or equal to zero, but there are significant adjustment lags: the error correction parameter is positive and well confirmed. As equation (5) suggests, the equilibrium impact of anticipated inflation is positive. The relatively weak initial effect of anticipated inflation may be because the impact of anticipated inflation on house prices may be variable over time since the effect of inflation on real after-tax bond and share yields varies with changes in the personal and corporate tax schedules. There is, nevertheless, strong support for our central hypothesis that a higher rate of anticipated inflation ultimately causes house prices to rise relative to other prices.

As our earlier discussion suggests, building societies' ability to capture savings flows has an important direct influence on *equilibrium* house prices. The initial impact appears to occur with about a two-quarter lag, but this impact is considerably magnified in equilibrium by complete portfolio adjustment. Outside of equilibrium, the actions by building societies to compete for funds in financial markets, can, however, depress house prices relative to other prices in the short term. For instance, if deposit rates are raised to reduce a fall in their share of financial in-

TABLE 1

PARAMETER ESTIMATES

(DEPENDENT VARIABLE: ΔPH_t)

PARAMETER COEFFICIENT OF*	β_1 $\Delta \ln S_{t-1}$	β_2 $\Delta \ln BS_{t-2}$	β_3 $\Delta \ln RM_{t-2}$	β_4 $\Delta \ln Y_t$	β_5 $\Delta \ln Y_{t-1}$	β_6 $\Delta \ln CH_t$	β_7 $\Delta \ln HH_t$	β_8 $\Delta \ln G_t$	β_8 $\Delta \ln LAR_t$
(a) (OLS)	0.14 (1.58)	0.015 (3.79)	−0.11 (1.82)	0.585 (5.57)	0.351 (2.86)	−0.064 (2.15)	0.143 (2.34)	0.015 (3.75)	—
(b) (IV)	0.146 (1.65)	0.015 (3.83)	−0.192 (2.57)	0.679 (5.72)	0.326 (3.06)	−0.075 (2.65)	0.091 (1.58)	0.016 (4.24)	—
(c) (IV)	0.163 (1.75)	0.014 (3.42)	−0.186 (2.44)	0.696 (5.69)	0.331 (3.01)	−0.075 (2.61)	0.094 (1.60)	0.016 (4.13)	0.039 (0.57)

PARAMETER COEFFICIENT OF	γ_1 $\ln HH_{t-1}$	γ_2 $\ln(S_{t-1/PH})_{t-1}$	γ_3 $\ln(BS_{t-2/PH})_{t-1}$	γ_4 $\ln(HH/CH)_{t-1}$	R^2	Standard Error	D-W	$Z(6)$
(a)	0.11 (4.20)	0.072 (3.07)	0.028 (5.76)	0.05 (5.29)	0.90	0.012	2.08	5.1
(b)	0.09 (3.88)	0.053 (2.57)	0.026 (5.91)	0.049 (5.65)	0.91**	0.011**	2.06	7.38
(c)	0.092 (3.78)	0.057 (2.55)	0.026 (5.65)	0.049 (5.56)	0.91**	0.011**	2.05	5.77

*t statistics in parentheses
**Based upon instruments

termediation, mortgage rates are usually also raised, so the immediate effect is to reduce house prices. However, to the exent that they eventually succeed in maintaining (or increasing) their share as a result of this action, *equilibrium* house prices will stay the same (or rise) relative to other prices.

On the basis of the effect of changes in the nominal mortgage rate, our evidence also supports the suggested temporary impact of debt service burden on relative house prices. It is consistent with Kearl's findings for the U.S. that increases in anticipated inflation, as reflected in changes in the mortgage rate, may initially decrease house prices relative to other prices (by "tilting" the real payment stream). In equilibrium, however, the opposite occurs.

We have found that house prices are quite sensitive to changes in the rate of net household formation attributable to demographic change, but in addition, this variable (HH) plays a central role in the ability of the model to track house price behavior. If it is omitted or replaced with the number of marriages there is evidence of misspecification.[14] (Its inclusion also makes the constant term insignificantly different from zero, so the constant was omitted from the estimation in table 1.) It appears, therefore, that our construct of net household formation purely attributable to age distribution changes, HH, may offer a satisfactory solution to the problem of incorporating demographic factors into housing models.

Using equation (18), we can determine the estimated parameters of our demand function for owner-occupied housing in equilibrium from the parameter estimates in table 1.

$$\ln P_H = 1.14 \ln HH + 0.67 \ln S + 0.33 \ln BS \qquad (19)$$

The impacts of changes in HH, S, and BS on the equilibrium real price of owner-occupied housing are clearly a large multiple of the initial, disequilibrium impacts of these variables. This implies that the portfolio adjustments take a considerable time, which is not unreasonable given the large transaction costs and search costs associated with adjusting one's holdings of housing assets.

Unanticipated government policies also influence the movement of house prices outside of equilibrium. Increases in the availability of home improvement grants tend to increase real house prices. Like Mayes, we also find that an increase in council house completions tends to reduce house prices by taking pressure off the owner-occupied sector. Additionally, however, we find (1) the impact of council housing production is related to the behavior of demographic trends and (2) changes in the local authority rent level appear to have had little impact on the demand for owner-occupied housing, as we expected.

Finally, real house prices were generally falling from the third quarter of 1973 until mid-1977. We were interested in knowing whether our model could predict that turning point. To find out we dropped the last six observations and reestimated the model over 1967:2 to 1976:4. Using either OLS or IV estimates we can track the turning point, and indeed can trace the behavior of house prices reasonably well in the postsample period with our model. A chi-square test on Z(6), which compares the forecast errors with the standard error of the regression, suggests that the parameters are stable (see table 1).

Implications

Although errors in measuring anticipated inflation and house prices may make us somewhat doubtful about the precise values of the parameters,[15] our qualitative hypotheses receive strong support, so the following qualitative conclusions appear to be fairly robust. We have found a positive link between expected inflation and house prices relative to the prices of other goods and assets. This arises in large part because the relative tax advantage to investing in owner-occupied housing increases with the expected rate of inflation. Can such a variable subsidy to housing be the intention of the legislators? It seems unlikely in the light of growing concern about house price rises. Moreover, it only began to matter when general price inflation became high and variable, and this occurred well after the tax on imputed rental income was removed in 1963.

An obvious way to weaken, if not break, the link between anticipated inflation and real house prices is to remove the tax favoritism afforded owner-occupied housing relative to other assets. As has recently been stressed again, this tax favoritism is not the tax relief on mortgage interest, but the failure to tax imputed housing income or capital gains on owner-occupied housing.[16] But in the presence of these two tax exemptions, mortgage interest relief deepens the subsidy to owner-occupied housing.

Removal of some (e.g., mortgage interest relief) or all of the tax advantages to homeowners would allow substantial tax reductions elsewhere.[17] These could be used to reduce the cash flow burdens of the new tax on returns from housing, especially among certain groups such as pensioner households. In the absence of comprehensive indexing of the tax system (so that taxes are paid on real rather than nominal net returns) complete removal of homeowners' tax privileges may, however, reduce housing demand in favor of consumption,[18] or in favor of more investment in other tax-favored assets, such as pension schemes. This may not be considered socially desirable.

As an alternative which maintains encouragement to housing investment, a direct subsidy or tax credit as a replacement for mortgage interest relief would weaken the link between the size of the housing subsidy, anticipated inflation, and real house prices for those with equity in their house and break it for those with 100 percent mortgages. If net housing income were also taxed the link would be broken for all households. The rate of subsidy also would be independent of marginal personal tax rates.

Inflation-indexing of the taxation of returns from other assets and of interest payment deduction would also break the link between expected inflation and the demand for owner-occupied housing. The retention of the tax exemption of housing returns, accompanied by indexation of the remainder of the tax system, would entail a relative tax advantage to owner-occupied housing dependent upon the personal tax rate but independent of the expected rate of inflation. Such comprehensive indexing is considerably less likely, however, than the proposals of the preceding paragraph.

We have also found evidence supporting our claim that the institutional framework of building societies and their tax treatment, which produce continuous rationing of mortgage funds at below market interest rates, entail a direct relationship between building societies' lending and real house prices. The Wilson Committee has recommended that the building societies' rate-setting "cartel" be abolished and the societies' tax advantages removed.[19] Together these recommended changes would tend to eliminate the interest rate gap and sever the *equilibrium* relationship between building society lending and real house prices.[20] Thnis can be illustrated using figure 2, which shows the market for mortgage funds (for a given expected rate of inflation).

The supply schedule S_0 represents the present supply function, and given the rate-setting function of the cartel, there is presently excess demand (of M_0M^*) at the mortgage rate RM_0. Opening up competition among building societies would tend to push up deposit rates and the mortgage rate to RM_1. Note that this tends to increase the amount of mortgage funds actually flowing into housing, thereby tending to raise house prices. Removal of building societies' tax privileges, however, shifts the supply schedule upward (say to S_1), which pushes up the mortgage rate further, but the end result may be either an increase or decrease of

FIGURE 2

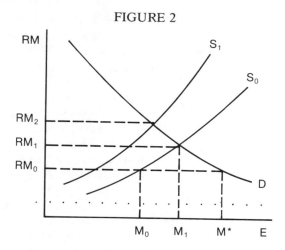

funds flowing into housing demand. In short-run equilibrium, real house prices would henceforth be a function of the *real* mortgage rate (but no longer BS) in addition to permanent income, net household formation, and expected inflation (if the tax reforms discussed above are not made).

According to our model, abolition of building societies' tax privileges and any reduction of the relative tax advantage to homeowners clearly tend to reduce real house prices, thereby entailing real capital losses to existing homeowners. Given the portfolio adjustment lags that we have found, the immediate declines may not, however, be dramatic. Moreover, as noted, opening up of competition among building societies provides an upward push to house prices, and over the next 10 years or so net household formation will also tend to push house prices up. So the real capital losses will tend to be distributed over a considerable period. Nevertheless, the shifts in monthly household financial burdens resulting from the suggested changes would tend to be large, thus suggesting that a "phasing in" of the changes would be required, as well as some offsetting tax reduction. By depressing the real price of houses, new home buyers would tend to gain from such changes, and, if as suggested, more savings flow into housing as a result of competiton among building societies (through higher deposit rates), first-time buyers would also benefit from the greater amount of mortgage finance available.[21] The substitution of a direct subsidy to housing for the present tax subsidy would, of course, reduce the real capital losses to existing owners.

In the more likely situation of no-change in the tax subsidy to owner-occupied housing, current antiinflationary policies also entail capital losses for homeowners to the extent they are successful in bringing down the inflation rate. Our analysis also indicates that government efforts to manipulate mortgage rates or the loan volume of building societies can have a major influence on house prices. Less immediately apparent, but following from our model, is that other housing policies such as home improvement grants and council house building significantly influence house price movements thus suggesting a more integrated approach to housing policies is necessary if the desired outcome is to be achieved.

There is a danger that since owner-occupation will appear to be less "affordable" in the sense that the ratios of monthly payments to income and down payments to income rise, pressure for subsidies may grow, as it has in the USA. This view ignores the financial asset aspects of owner-occupied housing stressed here. In this light, our model suggests that a request for additional subsidies (on top of the tax favoritism) can be seen as the case of subsidies begetting more subsidies. Although it must be noted that there probably are cash-flow barriers to house purchase for young couples, their elimination requires different policies from those meant to dampen "rising costs," such as different mortgage instruments, and we have indeed seen that removal of housing's tax subsidy would actually aid first-time buyers by lowering house prices and allowing general tax cuts.

Finally, the analysis in this paper has implications for modeling the housing market. We have already mentioned the inclusion of pure demographic factors. Our results also suggest that current income may not be having the type of effect it is generally thought to have in time series models of housing demand. The importance of permanent income in the demand for housing services is generally stressed; yet researchers continue to use current income (possibly with lags or moving averages) in their time series studies while it would only affect the *equilibrium* demand for housing if households were generally liquidity-constrained. Hall's (1978) theoretical analysis suggests that permanent income is relatively constant over the short periods of time generally employed in quarterly models (e.g., 10 years), exhibiting a gentle upward trend. In addition, our empirical results suggest that current income only has a temporary disequilibrium impact on the asset demand for housing, as you would expect transitory income to have. So the coefficients of income in other time series analyses of owner-occupied housing demand may merely reflect a combination of transitory income effects and spurious correlation. One may argue that if credit is rationed by building societies, households are also liquidity constrained, but that view ignores other sources of housing finance. Fluctuations in first-time buyers' loan-to-value ratios with building societies suggest they use other sources of finance when building society credit is less available.

The modeling exercise in this paper focused on the demand for owner-occupied housing. Discovery of the extent to which changes in real house prices are eventually moderated by supply responses requires that the supply side also be investigated. In the U.K. during recent years, the supply response of builders to house price changes has been sluggish. Indeed, this sluggish response has made it easier for us to estimate our demand function (see discussion of H/Q ratio above). But the formulation of housing policies requires that we also know the extent to which changes in the real house prices affect house building. In particular, to what degree have the dramatic fluctuations in real house prices themselves created a climate of uncertainty which has inhibited building responses to price changes?

Appendix

RPH The average price of dwellings mortgaged with building societies deflated by the implicit deflator of consumer expenditures 1970 = 100. The price comes from The Department of the Environment/Building Society Association 5% Sample Survey of Building Society Mortgages. The deflator is from *Economic Trends*.

LARENT An index of real local authority rents. Source: *Housing and Construction Statistics*.

INCOM Real personal disposable income in 1970 prices *Economic Trends*.

C Is an index of BSA/SAV.L/V where BSA is the net acquisition of assets by building societies; SAV is personal sector saving before providing for depreciation, stock appreciation and additions to reserves; L/V is the loan-to-value ratio on building society mortgages. Sources: *Financial Statistics* and *DOE/ BSA Survey*.

CH The completion of public sector dwellings in the U.K. lagged one quarter. Source: *Housing and Construction Statistics*.

All the above data were seasonally adjusted by the XII method.

HH   The change in the number of standardized households is the change in the number of households which would exist if the age/sex marital status-specific headship rates and marriage proportions observed in 1971 prevailed in all the observation period with the actual age/sex distribution of the population. Source: See Ermisch (1979) for a fuller discussion and the weighting scheme used. The change in the annual figures was interpolated quarterly and then smoothed by a 10-quarter moving average.

RMOR   The mortgage interest rate. Source: *Financial Statistics.*

GRT   Home Improvement Grants. Source: *Housing and Construction Statistics.*

S   Is the product of the basic tax rate and the yield on consols (based upon the assumption that the real, pretax rate of return is constant). Source: *Economic Trends.* A six-quarter moving average was used.

REFERENCES

Arcelus, F., and A. H. Meltzer. 1973. "The Markets for Housing and Housing Services." *Journal of Money, Credit and Banking* 5 (February): 78–99.

Artis, M. J.; E. Kiernan; and J. D. Whitley. 1975. "The Effects of Building Society Behaviour on Housing Investment." In M. Parkin and A. R. Nobay, eds. *Contemporary Issues in Economics.* Manchester University Press, pp. 37–62.

Atkinson, A. B., and M. A. King. 1980. "Housing Policy, Taxation and Reform." *Midland Bank Review* (Spring): 7–15.

Boskin, M. 1978. "Taxation, Savings and the Rate of Interest." *Journal of Political Economy* 86 (April): S3–S27.

Byatt, I. C. R.; A. E. Holmans; and D. E. W. Laidler. 1973. "Income and the Demand for Housing: Some Evidence for Great Britain." In M. Parkin and A. R. Nobay, eds. *Essays in Modern Economics.* London: Longman.

Davidson, J. E. H.; D. F. Hendry; F. Srba; and S. Yep. 1978. "Econometric Modelling of the Aggregate Time Series Relationship between Consumer Expenditure and Income in the United Kingdom." *Economic Journal* 88 (December): 661–692.

Department of the Environment. 1977. *Housing Policy, Technical Volume.* Part II, London: HMSO.

Ebrill, L. P., and U. M. Possen. 1978. *Inflation and the Taxation of Equity in Corporations and Owner-Occupied Housing,* Working Paper No. 174, Department of Economics, Cornell University, Ithaca, New York.

Ermisch, J. F. 1980. *An Economic Theory of Household Formation: Theory and Evidence from the British General Household Survey,* Working Paper. Policy Studies Institute, London.

Fair, R. C., and D. M. Jaffee. 1972. "Methods of Estimation for Markets in Disequilibrium." *Econometrica* 40 (May): 497–514.

Fama, E. 1975. "Short-Term Interest Rates as Predictors of Inflation." *American Economic Review* 65 (June): 269–282.

Feldstein, M. 1976. "Inflation, Income Taxes and the Rate of Interest: A Theoretical Analysis." *American Economic Review* 66 (December): 809–820.

———., and G. Chamerlain. 1973. "Multimarket Expectations and the Rate of Interest." *Journal of Money, Credit and Banking* 5 (November): 873–902.

———., and O. Eckstein. 1970. "The Fundamental Determinants of the Interest Rate." *Review of Economics and Statistics* 52 (November): 363–375.

———; Green; and E. Sheshinski. 1978. "Inflation and Taxes in a Growing Economy with Debt and Equity Finance." *Journal of Political Economy* 86 (April): S53–S70.

Haavelmo, T. 1960. *A Study in the Theory of Investment.* Chicago.

Hadjimatheou, G. 1976. *Housing and Mortgage Markets.* Farnborough (Hants): Saxon House.

Hall, R. E. 1978. "Stochastic Implications of the Life Cycle-Permanent Income Hypothesis: Theory and Evidence." *Journal of Political Economy* 86 (November): 971–987.

Hickman, B. G. 1974. "What Became of the Building Cycle?" In P. A. David and M. W. Reder, eds. *Nations and Households in Economic Growth.* London: Academic Press, pp. 291–314.

Hillebrandt, P. M. 1977. "Crisis in Construction." *National Westminster Bank Quarterly Review* (November): 47–55.

Holmans, A. E. 1970. "A Forecast of the Effective Demand for Housing in Great Britain in the 1970's." *Social Trends* (No. 1), London: HMSO.

Hughes, G. A. 1979. "Housing Income and Subsidies." *Fiscal Studies* 1 (November): 20–38.

Kearl, J. R. 1978. "Inflation and Relative Price Distortion: The Case of Housing." *Review of Economics and Statistics* 60 (November): 609–614.

———. 1979. "Inflation, Mortgages and Housing." *Journal of Political Economy* 87 (October): 1115–1138.

———., and F. Mishkin. 1977. "Illiquidity, the Demand for Residential Housing and Monetary Policy." *Journal of Finance* 32 (December): 1571–1586.

Keynes, J. M. 1937. "The General Theory of Employment." *Quarterly Journal of Economics* 51: 209–223.

Maurice, R. 1968. *National Accounts Statistics: Sources and Methods.* London: HMSO.

Mayes, D. G. 1979. *The Property Boom: The Effects of Building Society Behaviour on House Prices.* Oxford: Martin Robertson.

Rosen, H. S. 1979. "Housing Decisions and the U.S. Income Tax: An Econometric Analysis." *Journal of Public Economics* 11 (February): 1–24.

Saunders, A. 1979. "The Short-Run Causal Relationship Between U.K. Interest Rates, Share Prices and Dividend Yields." *Scottish Journal of Political Economy* 26 (February): 61–71.

Taylor, C. T., and A. R. Threadgold. 1979. *"Real" National Saving and its Sec-*

toral Composition. Discussion Paper No. 6, Economic Intelligence Department, Bank of England, London.

Tobin, J. 1961. "Money, Capital and Other Stores of Value." *American Economic Review* 51 (May): 26–37.

Whitehead, C. M. E. 1975. "Inflation and the New Housing Market." *Oxford Bulletin of Economics and Statistics* 35 (November): 275–293.

_____. 1974. *The U.K. Housing Market: An Econometric Model,* Farnborough (Hants): Saxon House.

Wilkinson, R. K. 1973. "The Income Elasticity of the Demand for Housing." *Oxford Economic Papers* 25 (November): 361–377.

[Wilson] Committee to Review the Functioning of the Financial Institutions. 1979. Chairman, H. Wilson. *Second Stage Evidence,* Vol. 3, London: HMSO.

_____. 1980. *Final Report,* Cmnd. 7937, London: HMSO.

5

THE PRICE OF HOUSING, 1950-1975: SYNOPSIS

Bruce W. Hamilton and Timothy W. Cooke

This work is an attempt to estimate the time path of the rental price of housing (both owner-occupied and rental) from 1950 to 1975. Our work does not make direct observations on rental prices; rather we set up a supply and demand model and assume that rent clears the market in each period. We then infer what the rent must have been, given data on the population and the housing stock. The demand side of the model assumes that housing services demanded depend upon income and the rental price. Given the size distribution of household income, we can compute a quality distribution of demand for housing, for any level of rental price. The supply side is characterized by constant returns in construction in any given year, and an assumption that housing units are putty-clay. Thus a dwelling unit of a given quality cannot economically be upgraded nor subdivided. The implication is that a housing market characterized by excess demand for high-quality housing and excess supply for low-quality housing cannot achieve equilibrium by upgrading the low-quality housing. The only option is to tear down the low-quality housing and construct new high-quality housing. The model is completed with a partial-

[The authors are assistant professor of economics, Johns Hopkins University, and graduate student, Johns Hopkins University, respectively.]

adjustment mechanism whereby a constant fraction of excess demand is satisfied by new construction in each year.

Qualitatively, the model leads to the observation that a society such as ours, with secularly rising income and a fairly stable population, will have a chronic shortage of high-income housing and a chronic surplus of low-income housing. Construction will occur at the upper tail of the house-quality distribution simultaneously with demolition at the lower tail.

The important data for the model are the value distribution of the standing stock of housing in 1950 and the size distribution of income in each year. Given the parameters of the demand function, we can map the size distribution of income into a distribution of house-rent demands. And given the initial-year rent-value ratio, this distribution can be mapped into value-demand space. In year 1, this information directly gives us excess demand by house-rent level, as can be seen in figure 1. Some fraction (to be estimated) of the excess demand is satisfied by construction, thereby altering the supply distribution for year 2. In addition, income shifts in year 2, shifting the demand distribution. The supply and demand distributions for year 2 give a new value for excess demand, a fraction of which will again be satisfied by new construction.

As can be seen, the model predicts number of dwelling units constructed in each year, given the values of the parameters and variables. In principle, the estimation problem is now straightforward—find the set of parameter values which minimizes the sum of squared prediction errors for housing starts. In fact, the estimation is a bit tricky, because the model

FIGURE 1

SIZE DISTRIBUTION OF HOUSE RENT DEMAND AND SUPPLY

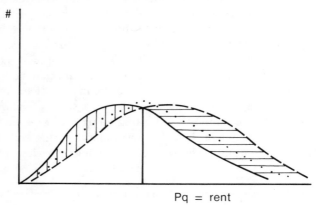

Pq = rent

takes the form of an algorithm (a simulation model, essentially) rather than a closed-form equation. So the search over the parameter space is considerably more labor intensive than in standard estimation problems. But we have managed to optimize the fit of the model using two different variables: housing starts (mentioned above) and average value of new dwelling units constructed (also predicted by the model, as can be seen from figure 1).

The time path of the dependent variables (which we try to explain with our model) can be summarized as follows: ignoring cycles, housing starts showed a mild upward trend through most of the period, punctuated by a huge burst of construction activity over the three-year period centered around 1972. Average real value of new dwelling units showed little trend, and its most impressive episodes were a trough in average value in 1972 and a huge peak in 1974.

Qualitatively, our model does a good job of predicting these time series with the following parameter values:

1. Housing demand inelastic with respect to income; (approximately .7)

2. Housing demand inelastic with respect to price; (approximately .6)

3. A rate of decline in the rental price of housing of at least 2½ percent per annum over the sample period.

It is easy to see, qualitatively, why the findings of (1)—(3) explain the data, and why any findings in contradiction of these would be difficult to reconcile with the facts. The combination of price decline and price inelasticity explains the failure of house values to rise over a period when average income almost doubled. The price decline further helps to explain the steady rise in construction even though there was a housing shortage resulting from World War II in the early years of the sample period. Income inelasticity also helps to explain the failure of house values to rise in the face of rising income. The failure of house values to rise could also be explained by price elastic demand and a price increase, but we would then have trouble explaining the buoyancy of housing starts in the latter part of the sample period. Also, if demand is elastic with respect to price, it is plausible that it would also be so with respect to income (it must be so unless the cross-elasticity is large). But if demand is elastic with respect to income, it is more difficult to explain the failure of house values to rise.

To repeat, our estimate is that the real rental price of housing declined about 2½ percent per annum over the sample period.

6

Discussions of Bruce W. Hamilton and Timothy W. Cooke, "The Price of Housing, 1950–1975: Synopsis"

Craig Swan, first discussant

This is certainly a provocative paper. This morning's discussion has indicated that. I also think it's an imaginative methodology. I'd be interested to see whether more mileage might come out of the Hamilton-Cooke methodology. I also agree with at least part of one of the major conclusions: recently the price of housing has been declining on some sort of secular basis. But at the same time it's not clear to me that the present version of the Hamilton-Cooke paper is a strong piece of evidence in favor of the conclusion. The rest of my remarks are highly critical of the actual data that Hamilton and Cooke use. Before being critical I want to again commend the authors for a new and imaginative approach to an important problem, an approach that with more appropriate data may provide us with valuable additional insights into the recent behavior of housing markets.

What exactly is meant in the paper by the price of housing? I would list four prices of housing—Pat listed three—we'll have an infinite number before we're through here. The present paper fails to make a clear distinction between these alternatives. As a result one can be led into some real problems. One way to measure the price of housing is to measure the asset

[The author is associate professor of economics, University of Minnesota.]

price, presumably the transaction price for an existing dwelling, i.e., what it sells for. Another measure of housing prices has to do with the construction costs of producing new units. In long-run equilibrium you'd expect asset prices and construction costs to be the same, but they wouldn't have to be at all points in time.[1] These are both stock concepts 50, 60, 80, or 100,000 dollars. A third measure of the price of housing is the price of the flow of services. Pat measured this price as the user cost of housing. I get four measures by distinguishing between the implicit price for owner-occupants and explicit rents for renters. Hamilton-Cooke fail to make a clear distinction about what they mean by the price of housing. The result is confusion at different points in the paper.

I have several problems with the data in the paper. One has to do with the value measure and secular movements in the ratio of single-family and multifamily starts that, I think, gives rise to an essentially spurious measure of average house value. If I correctly understand what Bruce has done, he measures house value by taking total residential construction and dividing by total starts. Total starts include both single-family homes and apartment buildings. Thus the value figure is an average of multi- and single-family units. Multifamily units have traditionally been significantly smaller than single-family homes. By itself this difference in unit size need not be a problem, but if there are life-cycle effects on the demand for housing that people adjust to by starting in apartments, moving to single-family homes, and perhaps ending up in apartments, then changes in the age structure of the population can introduce spurious movements into the Hamilton-Cooke value numbers.

In particular, during the sixties, with changing age structure of the population, multifamily homes rose as a proportion of total construction. Both single- and multifamily units could be going up in value, but Bruce's changing weights could keep his average figure constant. Then in the early part of the seventies there was a reversal of the single/multi trend. Bruce's procedure now puts a lot more weight back on the larger single-family homes. Thus it isn't surprising that his figures take a big jump. This jump need not parallel the movement in the average value of single- or multi-family units but is likely to merely reflect changing weights.

My second concern has to do with what I believe to be an essentially spurious cyclical component in the data. Hamilton and Cooke estimate per unit value by taking the value of residential construction during a calendar year and dividing by starts in the same calendar year. This procedure introduces spurious cyclicality because the value of residential construction during any one year is simply a mechanical weighted average of the value of previous starts. In a cyclical downturn, starts fall dramatically while construction stays up because one is still finishing the higher number of earlier starts. Dividing the value of construction by current starts will then show a sharp peak even if nothing has been happening to house values. These peaks in house values during credit crunches may simply be a reflection of this induced cyclicality, and attempts to explain this cyclicality may be misleading.

A third data concern that I have runs throughout the whole paper. The Hamilton and Cooke data show a tremendous housing boom that they need to explain. That is part of the reason they find a secular price decrease. Over the period real income and the number of households are both increasing but their measure of housing starts seems to increase more than can be explained by movements in income and household formation. I read the numbers somewhat differently. I looked at the ratio of housing starts to household formation over this period, and the ratio—that is, the number of new dwelling units started per additional household—has been declining. From 1950 to 1959 the ratio is about 1.6. During the sixties it drops to about 1.3. From 1970 to 1975 it has been about 1.1.[2] In terms of the number of starts I simply do not see a tremendous housing boom that needs to be explained. Where do Hamilton and Cooke get the numbers they use? If I look at their figure that shows housing starts, it appears that the numbers that they are using for the fifties are simply too low. While there are serious problems with starts data from the fifties the numbers that I'm familiar with average around 1.3, 1.4, 1.5 million. The Hamilton-Cooke numbers are substantially lower.[3] I do not understand the difference and wonder whether it contaminates the Hamilton-Cooke results.

I do not think that there is an empirical puzzle, but it's less clear to me that it is the one many people have in mind. In my mind the puzzle is not why have starts and construction remained so high in the seventies in the face of high nominal interest rates, but rather why haven't housing values risen even more?

If you look at the period 1966–1978, real per capita disposable income has increased by 35 percent. So as long as the income elasticity of the demand for housing is not zero one might expect a fairly substantial income effect. Ceteris paribus, an income elasticity of 1.0 would imply a 35 percent increase in quantity and, hence, deflated value. An elasticity of 0.5 would imply an increase of 17.5 percent. But if you look at Census data, the actual average value of new houses divided by the Census hedonic price index has only gone up by 9 percent. Increases in relative prices could clearly work to offset income effects, but the thrust of all the papers we've heard this morning is that the relative cost of housing services or the implicit price of housing has been declining, not rising. I wonder why average deflated value has not gone up even more.

If you look at structure prices, as measured by the ratio of the residential construction deflator to the GNP deflator over the same period, you find that relative structure prices have increased by 23 percent. The difference between 35 and 23 is 12 and that's pretty close to 9 on the assumption of unit elasticities of demand. If you use Bruce's estimates of less than unit elasticities of demand, estimates which are consistent with other recent evidence, you still get numbers that look pretty close to 9. Looking at structure prices seems to eliminate the puzzle, but it does so by using what appears to be the wrong price. The thrust of microeconomic considerations of household decision making indicates that one should look at the relevant user cost of housing capital when attempting to explain housing decisions, and that number, we are told, has been declining.

Anthony J. Sulvetta, second discussant

Hamilton-Cooke Model

The Hamilton-Cooke housing "price" model attempts to explain growth in the nation's housing stock between 1950 and 1975 concurrent with a decrease in stock "value levels." Their conclusions: increases in housing starts were too large to be explained by income growth and numbers of households; the value of new units increased moderately, while the "value level" of the stock declined. Possible explanations: growth in stock was due to decreases in relative price; new house values failed to appreciate significantly due to offsetting effects in price and quality; and stock outflow values offset new unit inflow values. Their results can be summarized as follows:

- house price (the cost of housing services) declined 3 percent per annum;
- "buoyant" housing starts appeared unrelated to income growth or household formation; and

[The author is director of economics studies, JRB Associates, Inc.]

- replacement rates, dependent on the rate of price change and rate of income growth, contributed to decreasing "value levels" of the standing stock.

This brief review of the model demonstrates that it fails to provide a basis for understanding past house price and value relationships, or for understanding future house price trends.

PROBLEMS WITH DEFINITIONS AND CONCEPTS

One difficulty in understanding the model presentation is the cumbersome and ambiguous use of terms—"average value," "house price," "value level," and "production costs"—for explaining the relative value of the existing stock, net additions to the stock, and cost of housing services. The "value level," if I interpret it correctly, is the net asset value of the stock which, according to Hamilton-Cooke, declined at roughly 3 percent per annum. House price, apparently gross production costs, remained near constant over time (increasing production costs were offset by quality increases). As the stock expanded, "value levels" declined due to exiting stock.

NONMALLEABILITY ASSUMPTION

At the center of the discussion is the nonmalleability assumption of the capital stock, giving rise to declining house price and implicit rents under conditions of rising incomes. The period is described as an opportune time for abandonment and demolition, with the exiting stock offsetting "value level" contributions of net additions. However, the nonmalleability assumption is questionable (probably unnecessary) if the basic point is that production costs, adjusted for quality improvements, lead to relatively stable "house prices."

Hamilton-Cooke's findings are readily duplicated by using residential construction cost data in constant 1972 dollars. Aggregating residential construction costs in five-year intervals between 1952 and 1972 and then dividing each interval by gross new starts show a small secular increase in costs per unit. Adjusting gross costs for quality improvements (using average floor space as a "quality" proxy) provides an estimate comparable with that derived in their model, a decline of 2.2 percent per annum. Combined with a 2 percent depreciation rate for abandonment and demolition (exiting stock), a decline of 3 percent per annum appears reasonable. Unfortunately, land costs are excluded from both analyses.

INCREASING VALUE LEVELS

Average gross production costs, unadjusted for land values and quality improvements, increased from $21.4 thousand (1952-1956) to $29.3 thousand per unit (1967-1972). If the cost of land is included, production costs rose moderately during the 1950s (approximately 18 percent); accelerated during the 1960s (increasing 27 percent); and during the inflationary environment of the 1970s (coupled with the baby boom entering the housing market), increased nearly 85 percent. With a 2 percent depreciation rate, three distinct periods are observed: (1) between 1950-1962, "value levels" remained relatively constant, a period characterized by low income and low adult population growth; (2) 1962-1972, a period of rapid income growth and emergence of the initial baby boom cohorts into the housing market—"value levels" started to increase; and (3) post-1972, an inflationary environment exacerbated by demands imposed by the formation of new households attributed to the baby boom cohorts—"value levels" accelerated.

BUOYANT HOUSING STARTS

Another questionable point made by the authors was that housing starts were "buoyant,"—too large to be explained by income growth and net new household formation. However, the evidence indicates that housing starts paralleled both population and income growth. For the decade of the 1950s, the percentage change in real disposable income per adult (in constant 1972 dollars) remained nearly constant; as indicated earlier, adult population growth was also relatively constant. As a result, net new household formation was low, possibly due to the shrinkage in cohorts ages 21 through 28 between 1952 and 1957, followed by moderate growth in these cohorts of about 3 percent between 1957 and 1962. Starts were far from buoyant. Average annual housing starts for the intervals 1952-1957 and 1957-1962 were 1.47 and 1.44 million units, respectively.

During intervals 1962-1967 and 1967-1972, the maturing baby boom cohorts (ages 21-28) emerged, increasing approximately 14.5 and 15.8 percent, concurrent with a 24 percent and 15.5 percent increase in real disposable income per adult. The foundation for a moderate boom in housing starts was established and materialized between 1967-1972 and 1973-1976. For the first period, starts increased to 1.55 million units per year; during the second period, to 1.69 million units per year. Net new household formation increased from 1.20 million units annually to 1.82 million units annually, indicative of a spreading out effect of new households within the existing stock.

Hamilton-Cooke's conclusion that buoyant housing starts were unrelated to income growth or household formation appears in error. For the period examined since 1952, housing starts appear both income and population sensitive—relatively constant with moderate growth in incomes and population during the 1950s and early 1960s and accelerating with income growth and the emergence of the baby boom cohorts into the housing market during the latter part of the 1960s through the mid-1970s.

CONCLUSIONS

Hamilton-Cooke's assertion that the value of the housing stock demonstrated a declining trend between 1952 and 1972, despite rapid growth in real per household income and stable population growth, is questionable. If "value level" refers to the value of services rendered by the stock over this period, then the price of services increased with increasing "house prices" as the stock expanded. It was demonstrated that for the period 1950–1972, conditions were dissimilar to those described by Hamilton-Cooke—"value levels" probably changed very little during the 1950s but accelerated during the 1960s. A take-off point becomes more obvious during the 1970s, when the income gains of the latter half of the 1960s and early 1970s, combined with a rapid expansion of the adult population, exerted sufficient demand pressures to stimulate housing production far above levels of the two preceding decades. The added element of inflation and the interaction between house price increases and interest rate deductibility provided a further impetus for rising prices, a self-fulfilling cycle. That the real cost of capital was declining and possibly even negative during the 1970s does not detract from the real level of housing services or "value level" of the stock. In short, and contrary to the Hamilton-Cooke model, the value of housing services rendered by the stock has been increasing and increasing at an increasing rate through the mid-1970s.

7

DEMOGRAPHIC TRENDS AND HOUSING PRICES

John L. Goodman, Jr.

When John Tuccillo asked me a few weeks ago to address this conference on the topic of demographic trends and their likely effect on housing prices over the next few years, I foolishly accepted before John told me that he would only give me 10 minutes to cover the topic. But then I thought maybe I could cover the topic in 10 minutes—with time to spare—for two reasons.

First, demographic trends aren't subject to much short-run fluctuation, only long-run change. Their effects on housing markets are most pronounced in the long run, whereas John wanted me to talk about the implications for housing prices over the next few years.

Second, the implications of demographic trends are clearer for the number of housing units that will be required and the location of those dwelling units than are the implications of demographic trends for the prices at which those units will sell. There have been several studies by Duane McGough and others at HUD and other studies in academia and industry in the past few years that look at the implications of demographic trends for types of housing units, number of housing units, and their locations over the next few years.

[The author is senior research associate, The Urban Institute.]

I had thought that one strategy would be simply to say that demographic trends will have little independent effect on housing prices and housing price changes over the next two-to-three years, and then yield my remaining time back to the chair. But I knew that in doing so, I'd run the risk of getting us close to back on schedule. Furthermore, it wouldn't be quite correct, since demographic trends, by affecting housing demand, must have some effect on housing prices unless supply is perfectly elastic. So, I'd like to use my remaining time to review very briefly some major demographic trends and raise some issues about the implications of these trends for housing prices over the next few years.

I'm extremely gun shy about even defining what I mean by housing price, given the discussion of this morning. I believe I'm referring to the asset price of owner-occupied housing, but I'm sure I'll be corrected several times in the subsequent discussion. Let me also say that I'm assuming throughout that demographic trends themselves are not likely to be substantially altered by anything short of an absolute collapse of the economy. Now I admit that this is a debatable point, but I think it is safe to say that the dominant direction of causality is from demographic events to economic conditions, rather than the other way around.

POPULATION CHANGE IN THE EARLY 1980s

First let me very quickly review the major demographic trends. I think most of you are familiar with these. I know of no forecast predicting a major break in the early 1980s from the demographic trends of the late 1970s that are the most relevant to housing market activity in general and housing prices in particular. Continued growth in the number of households nationwide (net household formations) seems a certainty over the next few years, probably at the annual rate of 1.5–2.0 percent. The rate of growth in households, of course, exceeds the rate of growth in population due to the decreasing average household size we're experiencing nationwide. This decrease in average household size means that even those metropolitan areas that are losing population at a fairly brisk rate will, by and large, not be losing households. Only 2 of the 25 largest metropolitan areas in the country declined in number of households during the first half of the seventies, whereas 8 of the 25 metropolitan areas declined in terms of population.

A second demographic trend is the shifting composition of households coming about because of rapid growth of non-husband/wife households. The importance here for housing markets is that husband/wife households have been the "bread and butter" of the owner-occupant market in the past. In 1977, they accounted for 75 percent of all homeowners, even though husband/wife households accounted for only 62 percent of all households.

A third trend concerns the location of population growth. No one is expecting a turnaround in migration trends out of the northeast and north central regions into the South and West, so there will be a continued relative growth in the number of households in the Sunbelt regions. The metro/nonmetro split, due to both spillover from formerly defined metropolitan area boundaries and through what we might call "hinterland resurgence," indicates that the rate of growth in number of households will be higher outside the metropolitan areas than in metropolitan areas. Within the metropolitan areas themselves, more rapid growth will occur in suburbs than in central cities.

IMPORTANCE OF THE SUPPLY SIDE

I mentioned at the outset that the effects of population change on housing prices are not straightforward. I convinced myself once and for all of this fact by looking at a few scatter plots last week of increases in asset value of owner-occupied houses against rates of growth in number of households for 39 metropolitan areas in the first two waves of the Annual Housing Survey. The distribution was completely random.

Clearly, supply conditions are at work and they determine how demographically induced demand changes get translated into a price change. Supply elasticities vary with the length of the adjustment interval. A market is more capable of absorbing 10 percent population growth if it occurs over a decade than if over a year. Supply elasticities also vary across markets, due to variations in building technology, land availability, and other development costs.

TRADE-UP BUYERS

Let me mention two less obvious demographic changes that I think will have some bearing on housing demand and, therefore, on housing prices over the next few years. The first is the increasing importance of trade-up buyers relative to first-time buyers as a percentage of all homeowners during the 1970s. (See table 1.) During the seventies there has been a slight increase in rates of home purchases, up about a percentage point on a base of either all movers or all households. But what is more noteworthy than this increasing importance of home purchasers is their identity. In 1973, only 40 percent of all people who bought and moved to homes owned homes before they made the move. In 1977, that figure was up to 48 percent, and the trend line is monotonic. There are plenty of people here who are more capable than I of spelling out the implications of that trend for housing demand and housing prices. But I think that the effect of the accumulated equity that these trade-up buyers bring back into the market with them has to be significant.

Before I looked closely at these numbers, I just assumed that the increase in repeat purchasers was merely a manifestation of the aging of the baby boom cohorts, but it's not at all. The increase is due instead to the selection of buyers from within each age group from which we have data available from the AHS. That is, compared to 1973, in 1977 a higher percentage of buyers within each age group were premove owners. The aging of the baby boom cohort has played little effect in this increasing importance of trade-up buyers. When you project the age distribution of household growth through the next few years up to 1985, it appears that the aging will have no effect in the future as well.

The recent increasing importance of trade-up buyers is not attributable to the aging of the baby boom cohort, nor will this continued aging play a role over the next few years.

RATE OF GROWTH AND THE COMPOSITION OF GROWTH

Finally, let me mention one other demographic fact that might not be too obvious. This regards the interaction between the rate of growth in number

TABLE 1

FIRST-TIME AND TRADE-UP HOMEBUYERS, BY AGE

Age of Household Head	Percentages of Homebuyers Who Are First-Time Buyers	Percentages of All Homebuyers In This Age Category, 1977	Projected Percentage Increase in Number of Households, 1977–85 (Series B)
<25	93.1%	9.6%	9%
25–29	52.0	15.2	23
30–34	39.3	19.7	29
35–44	28.1	28.6	37
45–64	18.7	20.3	2
65+	15.1	6.8	18
Total	37.2	100.0	17

Source: Public use file of basic records, 1977 Annual Housing Survey, and Current Population Survey, P-25, No. 807.

of households in a local market area and the composition of that growth. (See table 2.) As I mentioned, most metropolitan areas will continue to experience some growth in number of households over the next few years. But the difference between a 1 percent annual growth rate in number of households, say, for Cleveland and a 4 percent annual growth rate for Houston may actually understate the differences between those two market areas in growth of housing demand. That is, the doubling of the household growth rate may mean more than a doubling of the increase in housing demand.

The reasoning goes something like this. Growth in households occurs through two sources: redistribution among households of the population in an area already and net in-migration. The higher the growth rate of the number of households in a market, the more the growth is going to be occurring through in-migration of households. And growth through in-migration adds more to housing demand than does growth through natural increase. In-migrants are more often husband/wife households compared to growth that is "homegrown." In-migrants are more likely to be husband/wife households who bring with them their high homeownership propensities even if they do rent initially upon moving into the market area. Secondly, growth through in-migration tends to be of younger age groups.

TABLE 2

HOUSEHOLD COMPOSITION OF INTER-METROPOLITAN MIGRANTS, 1977, AND OF TOTAL METROPOLITAN GROWTH, 1970-77

Household Types	Inter-SMSA Migrants 1977	Total SMSA Growth 1970–77
Husband/Wife Families:		
Head less than 30 years old	15%	2%
30–64 years of age	32	9
65+ years of age	1	7
Single-Person Households:		
Under 65 years of age	27	30
65+ years of age	2	14
Other Households		
Under 65 years of age	22	37
65+ years of age	1	1
Total	100%	100%

SOURCE: 1977 Annual Housing Survey.

It is less likely to be growth of elderly households than is homegrown growth. Finally, when you look at numbers on reported house values of in-migrants and gross rents, it appears that in-migrants tend to both buy and rent toward the upper end of the market, independent of which tenure group they select. (See table 3.)

I would be happy to elaborate on any of these topics during the discussion period.

TABLE 3

House Values and Gross Rents

	Inter-SMSA Migrants, 1977	All SMSA Households, 1977
Median house value	$57,200	$40,600
Mean gross rent	224	193

Source: 1977 Annual Housing Survey.

8

INFLATION AND HOUSING COSTS

Ann Dougherty and Robert Van Order

Both the cost of buying a house and interest rates charged to finance housing have risen rapidly over the last few years. These increases have suggested, among other things, that housing is a major contributor to inflation and that "affording" a house is becoming more difficult.[1] On the other hand, people appear to have been buying houses in undiminished numbers, suggesting that they are affording them somehow.

This paper is a preliminary investigation into the measurement of the cost of housing. A more detailed and complicated discussion of trends in housing costs is contained in Villani (1979). Here we focus on two issues: a theoretical foundation for measuring the cost of housing and some estimates of how using our measure affects actual indices of housing costs and inflation generally. We argue that the Consumer Price Index (CPI) is significantly affected by using our measure and that the rise in housing costs has been greatly overstated.

There are two reasons for our results. The first is the failure to allow for the favored tax treatment of housing and the second is the failure to account for the (either implicit or explicit) capital gains coming from

[The authors are economists, U.S. Department of Housing and Urban Development.]

[ACKNOWLEDGMENT. The authors are grateful for comments from D. Diamond, E. Kane, P. Hendershott, J. Kau, J. R. Kearl, and K. Villani. What follows does not necessarily represent the views of the department.]

homeownership. The purpose of the theoretical section is to derive how these should be treated.

Our policy conclusions are strong. There is no "affordability" problem per se; homeownership is relatively cheap. There may be, however, a financial problem in that some borrowers cannot use future nominal income gains effectively and face a "cash flow" constraint. This problem requires nothing more than an appropriately graduated, or indexed mortgage. We consider some preliminary evidence, which suggests that whatever cash flow problem there is has not been significantly worsened by inflation.

Theory

We have in mind two approaches to measuring homeowner cost. The first, which might be classified "user cost" looks at household utility maximization. It then derives the expression for equating the marginal rate of substitution between housing and other goods to the relative cost of these two. We then multiply this by the price of other goods and call this the nominal cost of housing, which will take the form of standard user costs of capital assets.

The second approach, which might be classified as "implicit rent," views homeowners as profit maximizing landlords that rent to themselves. We then calculate, given the tax advantages that homeowners receive, the rent that would prevail in a competitive market.

Not surprisingly, the two approaches lead to the same result. We then compare these to the rent that a "real" landlord (given actual tax breaks) would charge and compare this with the homeowner index.

Assume there are two goods, owner-occupied housing (h) and non-durable consumer goods (c), with purchase prices (omitting time subscripts) p_h and p, respectively. The household can issue or buy bonds, whose real value is given by b, at nominal interest rate i. It pays an income tax on labor income, whose real value is y, and on nominal interest received. It also deducts any interest payments. The tax rate is given by θ and is fixed. Letting $q = p_h/p$, $Y =$ nominal income, $B =$ nominal value of bonds; and letting time be indexed by t, the household's current budget constraint is given by

$$pc_t + s_t + p_h\, x_t = (1 - \theta)Y + (1 - \theta)iB_t$$

or dividing both sides by p

$$c_t + s_t + qx_t = (1 - \theta)y + (1 - \theta)ib_t \tag{1}$$

where x_t and s_t are real gross housing purchases and real saving, respectively. They are defined by

$$h_{t+1} - h_t = x_t - dh_t \tag{2}$$

and

$$b_{t+1} - b_t = s_t - \pi b_t; \qquad \pi = \text{expected inflation rate} \tag{3}$$

where d is the rate at which houses depreciate (real bonds depreciate at the expected inflation rate). For simplicity we assume q and i to be constant.

Households maximize a standard utility function of the form

$$U(c_o, c_1, \ldots c_h; h_o, h_1, \ldots h_n)$$

subject to constraints (1), (2), and (3). We make no particular assumptions about U, except that we require that a solution exist. Form the Lagrangian

$$L = U(c_o, c_1, \ldots c_n; h_o, \ldots h_n) - \sum_0^n \lambda_t^1 (h_{t+1} - h_t - x_t + dh_t)$$

$$- \sum_0^n \lambda_t^2 (b_{t+1} - b_t - s_t + b_t)$$

$$- \sum_0^n \lambda_t^3 (c_t + s_t + qx_t - (1 - \theta)y_t - (1 - \theta)ib_t$$

Necessary conditions for an optimum are

$$U_{ct} - \lambda_t^3 = 0 \tag{4}$$

$$U_{ht} + \lambda_t^1 - \lambda_{t-1}^1 - \lambda_t^1 d = 0 \tag{5}$$

$$\lambda_t^2 - \lambda_{t-1}^2 - \pi\lambda_t^2 + \lambda_t^3 (1 - \theta)i = 0 \tag{6}$$

$$\lambda_t^1 - \lambda_t^3 q = 0 \tag{7}$$

$$\lambda_t^2 - \lambda_t^3 = 0 \tag{8}$$

along with the constraints (1), (2), and (3).

We can rewrite (5) as

$$\Delta\lambda^1 = d\lambda_1 - U_n \tag{9}$$

and (6) as

$$\Delta\lambda^2 = \pi\lambda^2 - (1 - \theta)i\lambda^3 \tag{10}$$

Then using (4), (7), and (8) to put all multipliers in terms of U_c we have (after substituting into (9) and (10))

$$[(1 - \theta)i - \pi + d] \, q = \frac{U_h}{U_c} \tag{11}$$

The right-hand side is simply the marginal rate of substitution of houses for consumer goods. The left hand-side is the ratio of the real after-tax cost of housing to p, the price of consumer goods. We contend that this is the appropriate measure of housing cost on the grounds that it is a measure of the dollar value to homeowners (in terms of marginal rate of substitution) of an additional unit of housing.

Note that (11) does not have any intertemporal aspects in it. In fact, it is easy to interpret our housing cost measure as a "rental" price (as will be seen shortly), suggesting that the effect of a rise in interest rates on housing is not through intertemporal effects as much as through ordinary relative price changes. Intertemporal effects do matter, as is seen by noting that (11) cannot be solved for a housing demand curve. It can be solved for h as a function of housing costs, and c, but c is endogenous. Presumably it depends on income, wealth, etc.; and it is here that intertemporal aspects enter, but they are no more essential to housing than to, say, food.

An alternative way of looking for the appropriate index is to ask what a landlord with similar tax breaks would charge in a competitive market. Such a landlord would wish to maximize (abstracting from operating costs) the present value of the "real" cash flow from renting houses. His tax break is that he can deduct interest expenses but does not pay a tax on rent. Thus, he maximizes

$$\sum_0^\infty (vh_t - qx_t) \, \frac{1}{(1 + r)^t} \tag{12}$$

where

$v = R/P$ (real rent)

$r = (1 - \theta)i - \pi$, the real discount rate

$R =$ nominal rent

subject to

$$h_{t+1} - h_t = x_t - dh_t \tag{13}$$

Substituting (13) directly into (12) and setting the first derivative equal to zero we have

$$0 = \left(\frac{1}{(1 + r)}\right) t - 1q_t + (v + q_t - q_t d) \frac{1}{(1 + r)^t} \tag{14}$$

Solving this gives

$$v = (r + d)q \tag{15}$$

or

$$R = [(1 - \theta)i - \pi + d]p_h \tag{16}$$

where R is nominal rent and p_h the purchase price of housing. For an arbitrary price of housing and arbitrary R this equation will not hold; which is to say that in such cases the amount of rental housing demanded by landlords will be either zero or infinite. In equilibrium, with a nonzero, finite amount of housing, R and p must be such that (16) holds, so that it can be considered an equilibrium equation for the rent that competitive landlords would charge. It tells the same story as (11) above.

Hence, whether we look at housing from the standpoint of a household expressing its preferences over time or a landlord renting the unit (to himself) we get the same index for homeownership costs.

This measure is not at all the same as that used, for instance, in the Consumer Price Index (CPI), which looks at both house price by itself and interest payments (ip_h). In fact, the two measures can be expected to move in opposite directions. Rewriting (11) or (16) our measure of homeownership cost is given by

$$[(1 - \theta)(i - \pi) - \theta\pi + d] \, p_h \tag{11'}$$

Consider the term in brackets. The first term is proportional to the "gross" real rate. Suppose, for empirical rather than theoretical reasons, that this gross real rate is constant. Then a rise in inflation will lower the term in brackets in (11') (our "cost of capital"), but it will raise nominal interest. Hence, depending on how house prices move, a period of inflation might involve the CPI measure rising rapidly and our measure falling.

The equation leads to the following observations:

1. Equation (11) can be integrated to show that the real price of a house (q) must equal the present value of U_h/U_c (the "imputed rent") discounted at the homeowner's cost of capital.

2. If we allow house price inflation to differ from inflation generally, then the expected rate of inflation in (11) is the rate of house price inflation, but the expected rate of inflation in discounting future imputed rents is the general rate of inflation.

3. It is expected future inflation that matters, actual inflation not being directly relevant.

4. Tax advantages belong in the index. For instance in a competitive market with landlords receiving homeowner tax advantages, the tax advantage would show up in the rent index.

5. The nominal rate of interest *is not* used in the nominal cost of capital. The nominal cost of capital is the *real* rate (adjusted for taxes) times nominal price, and the real cost is the same rate times *real* price. Hence, the equation does not support the notion that currently high nominal interest rates have had just a once and for all cost push effect (since after-tax real rates have probably fallen).

6. With transactions cost the holding period of the homeowner becomes relevant and the appropriate measure in (11) should be the average expected rate of house inflation over that period.

7. As has been pointed out elsewhere [e.g., Feldstein, Green, and Sheshinski (1978)], there is an important money illusion in the system due to the taxation of nominal interest. This is the major factor in the results that follow.

Of some interest is the relationship of this index (an imputed rent index) to an actual rent index. Clearly, there are tax differences that matter. For instance, landlords are more likely to pay capital gains taxes. They also pay tax on rents and can deduct depreciation for tax purposes. The depreciation has two interesting aspects: housing is evaluated at historical rather than current prices, and depreciation rates for tax purposes are larger than physical depreciation rates.

Taking these tax differences into account, a "real" landlord maximizes [following Feldstein, Green and Sheshinski (1977) and Boadway and Bruce (1978)]

$$\sum_{0}^{\infty} \left(\frac{1}{(1+r)} \right)^t ((1 - \bar{\theta})vh_t - qx_t - \alpha\, qh_t + \bar{\theta}dh_t{}^*q_t)$$

$$\begin{cases} \alpha = \text{effective tax rate on capital gains} \\ \bar{\theta} = \text{ordinary tax rate applicable to landlords.} \end{cases} \qquad (17)$$

where h_t* is the "accounting" value of the housing stock divided by p, d*
is the depreciation rate used for tax purposes. The constraints are

$$h_{t+1} - h_t = x_t - dh_t \tag{18}$$

$$h^*_{t+1} - h_t* = x_t - (d* + \pi)h_t*. \tag{19}$$

equation (19) reflects the notion of "accounting" stock, the d* reflecting
tax law depreciation (as opposed to "d," the actual rate) and our inflation
rate reflecting the "money illusion" from valuing at historical prices.

The manipulations involved in carrying out the optimization by landlords are tedious, and since essentially the same problem is worked out in
Van Order and Villani (1979) we simply assert that working out the
necessary conditions implies the result in Van Order-Villani

$$(- \bar{\theta})v = q \left(i(1 - \bar{\theta}) - (1 - \alpha)\pi + (1 - \bar{\theta})d \right.$$
$$\left. + \frac{\bar{\theta}r(d - d*) + \bar{\theta}d\pi}{r + d* + \pi} \right) \tag{20}$$

This equation is similar to that in Feldstein, Green, and Sheshinski
(1978). The final term, in the brackets, gives the subsidy (if d* > d) from
using the wrong depreciation rates and the cost in a period of inflation
from using historical cost.

To simplify, assume d = d*. Then (20) can be rewritten

$$v = (i - \gamma\pi + d + \sigma\pi)q \tag{21}$$

where $\gamma = (1 - \alpha)/(1 - \bar{\theta})$ and $\sigma = \bar{\theta}d/(r + d + \pi)(1 - \theta)$

Assume that a unit of housing has the same purchase price regardless of
whether it is rented or owner-occupied. Then the ratio of our imputed rent
index to this rental index is given by

$$I = \frac{(1 - \theta)i - \pi + d}{i - \gamma\pi + d + \sigma\pi} \tag{22}$$

or

$$I = \frac{(1 - \theta)(i - \pi) - \theta\pi + d}{i - \pi + (1 - \gamma + \sigma)\pi + d} \tag{22'}$$

For the rent index to be a good proxy for the homeowner cost index it is
necessary that I be invariant to changes in the rate of inflation. Suppose
initially that the after-tax real rate is invariant to changes in the rate of in-

flation, and that landlords and homeowner have the same tax rate. Then a rise in the rate of inflation will not affect the numerator but will raise the denominator. That is, the rent index overestimates[2] the homeownership index when inflation is increasing.

However, it would appear that, in fact, i has not adjusted by enough to keep after-tax real rates constant, and a better approximation is to assume that the gross real rate is constant. Under this assumption the effect of the rate of inflation on I is ambiguous. While landlords "lose" due to capital gains taxes and historic depreciation, they deduct depreciation, making the sign of the partial derivative ambiguous. Furthermore, if landlords, as we might expect, are in higher brackets, then the rent index may well fall relative to homeowner costs.

Before continuing, some comments are in order. The most obvious one is that capital markets are not perfect. One version of the problem is that borrowing (mortgage) rates and lending rates (opportunity cost on equity) are not equal. It can be shown that if, for instance, we add to the household optimization problem an equality constraint that fixes the loan-to-value ratio, then the appropriate "i" is the weighted average of the borrowing and lending rates. If the constraint is an inequality, the analysis is more complicated, but in the long run the appropriate rate will simply be the cheaper one. In any event, we doubt that movements in the difference between these are a major factor in housing costs.

Of potentially more interest is the possibility of constraints on total borrowing. The model above implicitly assumes that individuals can borrow large amounts in the early years of owning a house. In principle, there is no reason for this not to be the case since their wealth would be rising to cover the debt. Furthermore, the "borrowing" may simply take the form of drawing down initial wealth holdings or saving less than otherwise.

Nonetheless, solving the above problem may require more borrowing than capital markets actually allow consumers to borrow. Suppose we add a constraint $b \geq \bar{b}$ to the household maximization (of course $\bar{b}$ can be negative). It is straightforward to show that the new measure of ownership cost is

$$[(1 - t)i - \pi + d + \Delta]q \tag{23}$$

The last term in the bracketed expression represents the well-known "cash flow" constraint [see Kearl (1978)]. If borrowing is required to take a form that does not allow negative amortization and if interest rates rise as inflation rises, then the effect of inflation on housing demand is ambiguous. We shall return to this issue later.

Another issue recently raised by Douglas Diamond (1979) concerns the rate of the standard deduction. The "θ" used above is the representative homeowner's marginal tax rate. But the tax system is quite nonlinear. In particular, homeowners do not get a tax break on interest deduction between the standard deduction and the amount they deduct other than mortgage interest. Diamond (1979) computes estimates of housing costs adjusting for this. Since the standard deduction has been rising recently, the incentive to own rather than rent (especially for lower income groups with fewer other deductions) is diminished somewhat.

To some extent, Diamond's measure is of average cost—since for the homeowner currently itemizing deductions the adjustment is all water under the bridge. For our purposes—an index meant to be the argument in a demand function—our measure is probably the relevant one. From a "welfare" point of view, Diamond's may be appropriate. It is also useful in explaining tenure choice. It is clear from our measure of housing costs that inflation such as that of late should raise house prices. But Diamond's analysis suggests that homeownership (especially among low-income groups) need not change, with existing homeowners bidding up prices and renters not changing their behavior.

Finally, it should be pointed out that the tax advantage to homeownership is not just for deducting mortgage interest but includes the implicit deduction for equity (since the return on equity would be taxed). Some insight into the size of the tax break can be had from rewriting (11) again as

$$[(i - \pi)(1 - \theta) - \theta\pi]q \tag{11'}$$

If we assume (again for empirical more than theoretical reasons) that the gross real rate is constant in the long run, then housing cost fluctuations are due to changes in the relative price of housing and the rate of inflation and the product of these, and the tax rate is the tax subsidy to homeownership due to "money illusion." Note for instance that if inflation $= 8$ percent and the tax rate $= .25$, their product $= 2$ percent, which is on the order of magnitude of the real rate.

Numbers

In this section, we present some estimates of homeownership costs and the CPI, using alternative measures of homeowner cost. The basic measure of "finance cost" is equation (11), and the basic problem is the estimate of expected inflation. Not surprisingly, estimates are very sensitive to assumptions about the rate of inflation. The real after-tax rate is a number on the order of 2 percent per year; hence, a small error in inflation, say 1 percent, can lead to large (50 percent) error in finance costs. We also consider the CPI using only the rent index as a measure of homeowner cost.

HOW THE CPI HOMEOWNERSHIP
COMPONENTS ARE MEASURED

Currently, the CPI homeownership index is the weighted average of home purchase price, financing costs, taxes and insurance, and maintenance and repairs. Current weights for these elements were derived from the 1972–1973 Consumer Expenditure Survey and were incorporated into the index in the December 1977 revision. In between major revisions, the weights are moved by the relative price changes of the elements.

Homeownership is currently about 24 percent of the CPI, home purchase price 10 percent, and mortgage interest costs 7 percent. The mortgage interest cost index is the amount of interest contracted for on a "standard" house over the first half of the term of the mortgage. It is moved by the home purchase index and the mortgage interest rate index. The home purchase price index is calculated from FHA 203(b) program data, attempting to hold quality change constant. It is recognized that even though FHA price movements are probably similar to movements for conventional homes, the FHA data actually used are still a poor substitute[3] for conventional house prices. In addition, the CPI Home Purchase Index moves very differently from the Commerce Department's measure of a constant quality house even though they ostensibly measure the same thing.[4] The mortgage interest rate index is obtained from Federal Home Loan Bank Board (FHLBB) data and is also controlled for differences due to characteristics.

Before continuing, it should be noted that the homeownership index counts house price twice, once explicitly in its index of house price (which, again, is 10 percent of the CPI) and implicitly in the mortgage interest cost (7 percent of the CPI). Our measure implies that the first index does not belong at all. Hence, while the house price index has probably been biased downward, compared to actual house price movements, it has risen faster than our measures of homeowner cost so that its inappropriate use as 10 percent of the CPI has probably biased the index upward.

The rest of the homeownership part of the CPI is made up of maintenance, insurance, and other cost. We do not change these at all, focusing only on the finance part.

A major problem in calculating the CPI is the weights attached to the house price and mortgage interest cost parts (currently 17 percent of the 24 percent that is homeownership). These are changed by the relative price changes of the components. Since our measure will suggest that these have risen too rapidly, the weights used must also be too high. Rather than recalculate the weights every period, we have simply (and arbitrarily) set finance costs at 10 percent of the CPI.[5]

Hence, our numbers take out the 10 percent of the CPI that is its house price index and the 7 percent that is its mortgage interest cost and replace it with our estimate of equation (11) (assuming $\theta = .25$) as 10 percent of the index. The other weights are adjusted, so that all weights add up to 100 percent and relative rates remain constant. Since the maintenance and repairs part of the index does not explicitly include depreciation, we include it as part of finance costs, assuming a constant 1 percent rate.

Again, the major issue is the expected inflation rate. We have three candidates for measures. The first uses the nominal mortgage rate minus an estimate of the real mortgage rate (1.09%). The real mortgage rate was taken to be constant over the period and given by the average of the mortgage rate minus the inflation rate in a constant quality house over the period. This measure of expected inflation is given semiannually in column 1 of table 1.

The second estimate uses the long-term government bond rate minus a real rate (.82%). The real rate is estimated by subtracting the inflation rate from the bond rate and taking the average over the 1963–1978 period. It is given by column 2 in table 1.

Both of the measures are sensible in the sense that we should expect nominal rates to reflect expected inflation, but they are also unsatisfactory. Bond rates reflect general inflation rather than house price inflation and may reflect expectations that are not those of homeowners. Mortgage rates have been subject to various forms of policy aimed at controlling them and, therefore, may be very imperfect measures. In both cases the calculation of the real after-tax interest rate (given by columns 4 and 5 in table 1) must assume a constant gross (before-tax) real rate, and we have reason to believe that this rate has fallen.

One alternative measure of expected inflation is simply to use a weighted average of actual past changes in the inflation rate. We chose a similar but more complicated procedure. From Carlson (1977), we have semiannual data on expected inflation from surveys of consumers; but the paper does not give expected house price inflation, and it only gives expectations for six months or one year (which is shorter than the period relevant for a typical homeowner).

To take advantage of the information about expected inflation we

TABLE 1

ESTIMATES OF EXPECTED INFLATION AND AFTER-TAX REAL INTEREST COSTS

	E1[a]	E2[b]	E3[c]	C1D[d]	C2D[e]	C3D[f]
1967:1	5.313	3.755	1.971	0.489	0.676	3.831
1967:2	5.450	4.310	2.507	0.455	0.538	3.398
1968:1	5.948	4.453	2.052	0.330	0.502	4.226
1968:2	6.215	4.427	3.270	0.264	0.508	3.209
1969:1	6.742	5.078	2.944	0.132	0.345	3.929
1969:2	7.198	5.515	4.695	0.018	0.236	2.521
1970:1	7.382	5.872	3.822	−0.028	0.147	3.532
1970:2	7.088	5.638	3.654	0.045	0.205	3.479
1971:1	6.525	5.033	2.493	0.186	0.357	4.219
1971:2	6.628	4.815	3.602	0.160	0.411	3.186
1972:1	6.462	4.833	3.536	0.202	0.407	3.127
1972:2	6.573	4.798	3.098	0.174	0.415	3.649
1973:1	6.775	5.343	3.966	0.124	0.279	2.932
1973:2	7.405	5.628	4.686	−0.034	0.208	2.685
1974:1	7.827	6.023	6.160	−0.139	0.109	1.528
1974:2	8.130	6.302	5.318	−0.215	0.040	2.597
1975:1	7.833	6.018	5.844	−0.141	0.110	1.849
1975:2	7.890	6.338	6.707	−0.155	0.030	1.028
1976:1	7.885	6.078	5.477	−0.154	0.095	2.255
1976:2	7.945	5.865	5.699	−0.169	0.149	2.078
1977:1	7.900	6.235	5.984	−0.158	0.056	1.759
1977:2	8.047	6.248	6.913	−0.194	0.053	0.940
1978:1	8.432	6.895	7.195	−0.290	−0.109	0.946
1978:2	8.977	7.245	7.479	−0.427	−0.196	1.071
1979:1	9.627	7.617	8.964	−0.589	−0.289	0.073
1979:2	10.693	8.227	8.757	−0.856	−0.442	1.080

a. Expected inflation rate, using mortgage rate − 1.09.
b. Expected inflation rate, using government bond rate − 0.82.
c. Expected inflation rate, using forecast described in text.
d. After-tax real interest cost plus 1 percent depreciation ($\theta = .25$) using E^1.
e. After-tax real interest cost plus 1 percent depreciation using E^2.
f. After-tax real interest cost plus 1 percent depreciation using E^3.

estimated an equation designed to explain expectation formation. We
assumed that inflation expectations were formed by a simple distributed
lag of past actual inflation. From 1961–1975 (semiannually) the estimate
of this equation was

$$\pi = -.24 + .49\,\bar{\pi}_{-1} + +.10\,\bar{\pi}_{-2} + -.05\,\bar{\pi}_{-3} - +.12\,\bar{\pi}_{-4} \qquad (24)$$
$$+ .18\bar{\pi}_{-5} + .04\bar{\pi}_{-6}$$

We assumed that house price expectations were formed in the same way as prices generally, so that (24) could be used to forecast house prices by plugging house price data into it. We then obtained an expected rate for five years, using (24). This was done by using (24) every period to make forecasts semiannually for five years. The average of these forecasts is our estimate of expected inflation and is recorded in column 3 of table 1. The house price data used come from the Commerce (C-27) index of the price of a constant quality house. The index is given in column 2 of table 5, and the after-tax real rate using this measure of expected inflation (column 3) is given in column 6.

While the magnitudes of the three estimates of after-tax real rate differ (C_1 and C_2 being negative generally), they move in roughly the same direction, all indicating a significant decline in real capital cost. We are inclined to prefer C_3, but we make calculations using all three.

Table 2 gives homeownership costs. The last three columns are given by a weighted average of finance cost (real after-tax interest times house prices) and the other nonfinance items in the homeownership component, column 3 uses C_1, column 4 uses C_2, and column 5 uses C_3. The first column gives the rent index in the CPI and the second column gives the homeowner cost index actually used in the CPI. The differences are rather striking. The CPI, which uses nominal interest rates, indicates very large increases in homeowner costs, whereas the alternative three measures indicate not only that *nominal* costs have fallen, but they they may be negative.

Table 3 calculates the overall CPI using the homeowner cost indices in table 2. Comparing the first column, the published CPI, with the others reveals a very wide range of differences. The third and fourth columns, which use nominal interest rates for expected inflation, give clearly extreme results. We list them to illustrate the sensitivity of our measure of changes in measurement which, while not to be preferred, are not obviously silly. Our preferred measure (column 5), using C_3 the autogressive forecast, suggests that prices may have risen by a good deal less than is generally believed. Of the 112.5 percent rise in the CPI since 1967 our index suggests that about a quarter is spurious.

Table 4 calculates homeownership costs and CPI by different tax bracket. As is suggested by equation (11) the results vary significantly by tax bracket. This suggests an "unintended" regressiveness in the tax system. At low inflation rates, the tax break to different bracket owners may be what was "originally" intended as fair. But as inflation increases, the difference in treatment becomes much larger.

TABLE 2

Indices of Homeowner Costs: $\theta = .25$

	RENT[a]	CPIHOWN[b]	HO1D[c]	HO2D[d]	HO3D[e]
1967:1	1.000	1.000	1.000	1.000	1.000
1967:2	1.010	1.019	0.973	0.879	0.944
1968:1	1.021	1.042	0.840	0.873	1.120
1968:2	1.037	1.090	0.772	0.903	0.969
1969:1	1.051	1.141	0.617	0.766	1.149
1969:2	1.072	1.200	0.469	0.666	0.911
1970:1	1.094	1.267	0.415	0.582	1.132
1970:2	1.118	1.325	0.544	0.666	1.139
1971:1	1.146	1.333	0.790	0.876	1.336
1971:2	1.169	1.366	0.781	0.979	1.173
1972:1	1.187	1.398	0.877	1.004	1.197
1972:2	1.208	1.429	0.856	1.048	1.352
1973:1	1.235	1.449	0.794	0.899	1.234
1973:2	1.264	1.512	0.524	0.832	1.231
1974:1	1.295	1.592	0.330	0.709	0.974
1974:2	1.329	1.702	0.194	0.636	1.308
1975:1	1.363	1.803	0.348	0.773	1.154
1975:2	1.398	1.864	0.328	0.661	0.952
1976:1	1.435	1.909	0.344	0.805	1.365
1976:2	1.474	1.959	0.316	0.936	1.365
1977:1	1.519	2.020	0.323	0.775	1.307
1977:2	1.566	2.114	0.217	0.795	1.071
1978:1	1.619	2.216	−0.093	0.443	1.099
1978:2	1.678	2.369	−0.588	0.217	1.188
1979:1	1.729	2.524	−1.316	−0.134	0.694
1979:2	1.809	2.772	−2.416	−0.617	1.148

a. CPI rent index.
b. CPI index of homeowner cost.
c. Homeowner cost using C1 in table 1.
d. Homeowner cost using C2 in table 1.
e. Homeowner cost using C3 in table 1.

Regressions

Since our argument is that our measure of homeowner cost is justified by appeal to demand theory, it would seem appropriate to see if, in fact, it explains demand. A straightforward test would be to estimate a demand curve for housing, using our cost variable and other (income wealth, demographic data, etc.) variables to see if our measure is significant and alternatives are not.

TABLE 3

ALTERNATIVE MEASURES OF THE CPI

	CPI[a]	CPIR[b]	CPi1[c]	CPI2[d]	CPI3[e]
1967:1	1.0000	1.000	1.000	1.000	1.000
1967:2	1.0183	1.017	1.010	0.992	1.005
1968:1	1.0390	1.037	1.004	1.007	1.053
1968:2	1.0643	1.057	1.009	1.030	1.043
1969:1	1.0922	1.080	1.002	1.024	1.095
1969:2	1.1252	1.107	1.001	1.028	1.076
1970:1	1.1590	1.133	1.015	1.030	1.139
1970:2	1.1891	1.158	1.058	1.072	1.161
1971:1	1.2128	1.185	1.121	1.131	1.216
1971:2	1.2352	1.206	1.136	1.166	1.203
1972:1	1.2534	1.221	1.165	1.184	1.220
1972:2	1.2756	1.242	1.178	1.208	1.264
1973:1	1.3134	1.282	1.202	1.214	1.278
1973:2	1.3728	1.338	1.204	1.250	1.326
1974:1	1.4478	1.407	1.233	1.288	1.343
1974:2	1.5348	1.485	1.278	1.342	1.471
1975:1	1.5976	1.537	1.353	1.415	1.491
1975:2	1.6575	1.595	1.399	1.443	1.504
1976:1	1.6972	1.633	1.433	1.500	1.608
1976:2	1.7446	1.680	1.466	1.562	1.647
1977:1	1.8045	1.718	1.521	1.585	1.690
1977:2	1.8605	1.763	1.544	1.629	1.689
1978:1	1.9271	1.816	1.543	1.615	1.747
1978:2	2.0182	1.887	1.525	1.638	1.829
1979:1	2.1250	1.966	1.494	1.666	1.836
1979:2	2.2648	2.068	1.408	1.677	2.020

a. Actual CPI.
b. CPI replacing homeownership with rent index.
c. CPI replacing home purchase and mortgage interest costs with C1D·Houseprice from tables 1 and 5.
d. CPI replacing home purchase and mortgage interest costs with C2D·Houseprice from tables 1 and 5.
e. CPI replacing home purchase and mortgage interest costs with C3D·Houseprice from tables 1 and 5.

The alternative hypothesis, implied by the CPI, is that the nominal interest rate matters. A justification for its importance can be found in work [e.g., Kearl (1979)] that emphasizes the "tilt" effect of the fixed payment mortgage, which has until recently been the only one widely allowed in the United States. In a period of inflation, the high nominal interest rates tilt the profile of "real" mortgage payments, making them larger in the early

TABLE 4

HOMEOWNERSHIP COST INDICES FOR DIFFERENT TAX BRACKET (USING C^3)

	HO3D0[a]	HO3D[b]	HO3D50[c]	CPI30[d]	CPI3[e]	CPI350[f]
1967:1	1.000	1.000	1.000	1.000	1.000	1.000
1967:2	0.971	0.944	0.876	1.010	1.005	0.991
1968:1	1.118	1.120	1.124	1.052	1.053	1.054
1968:2	1.031	0.969	0.810	1.054	1.043	1.012
1969:1	1.190	1.149	1.044	1.102	1.095	1.076
1969:2	1.051	0.911	0.503	1.101	1.076	1.006
1970:1	1.220	1.132	0.904	1.155	1.139	1.096
1970:2	1.221	1.139	0.928	1.175	1.161	1.120
1971:1	1.356	1.336	1.286	1.219	1.216	1.208
1971:2	1.263	1.173	0.941	1.219	1.203	1.159
1972:1	1.287	1.197	0.964	1.236	1.220	1.176
1972:2	1.414	1.352	1.191	1.275	1.264	1.235
1973:1	1.358	1.234	0.916	1.300	1.278	1.217
1973:2	1.408	1.231	0.777	1.357	1.326	1.239
1974:1	1.266	0.974	0.223	1.396	1.343	1.196
1974:2	1.540	1.308	0.711	1.512	1.471	1.355
1975:1	1.449	1.154	0.396	1.544	1.491	1.343
1975:2	1.331	0.952	−0.024	1.573	1.504	1.312
1976:1	1.647	1.365	0.639	1.659	1.608	1.468
1976:2	1.681	1.365	0.553	1.703	1.647	1.489
1977:1	1.673	1.307	0.364	1.755	1.690	1.506
1977:2	1.559	1.071	−0.186	1.777	1.689	1.443
1978:1	1.640	1.099	−0.295	1.844	1.747	1.475
1978:2	1.796	1.188	−0.377	1.938	1.829	1.525
1979:1	1.523	0.694	−1.441	1.986	1.836	1.418
1979:2	1.967	1.148	−0.964	2.167	2.020	1.610

a. Homeownership cost comparable to HO3D in table 2 with $\theta = 0$.
b. Homeownership cost comparable to HO3D in table 2 with $\theta = .25$.
c. Homeownership cost comparable to HO3D in table 2 with $\theta = .50$.
d. CPI comparable to CPI3 in table 3 with $t = 0$.
e. CPI comparable to CPI3 in table 3 with $t = .25$.
f. CPI comparable to CPI3 in table 3 with $t = .50$.

years of the mortgage. As discussed, in the absence of "perfect" capital markets (i.e., a limit on the ability to borrow against future income) this cash flow problem will constrain demand, so that nominal interest could enter housing demand.

In terms of the analysis of the first section, if there is an upper limit on borrowing, then inflation should make the constraint more binding as inflation and nominal rates rise. That is, the cash flow constraint in (23) is a function of i.

TABLE 5

BASIC DATA

	Fore-cast[a]	House—price[b]	%CHS (House-price)[c]	Mort-gage rate[d]	Mainte-nance, tax, and Insur-ance[e]
1967:1	1.971	24.75	NA	6.403	1.000
1967:2	2.507	25.00	2.0	6.540	1.028
1968:1	2.052	25.95	7.6	7.038	1.057
1968:2	3.270	26.50	4.2	7.305	1.092
1969:1	2.944	28.00	11.3	7.832	1.129
1969:2	4.695	28.60	4.3	8.288	1.171
1970:1	3.822	29.20	4.2	8.472	1.207
1970:2	3.654	29.15	−0.3	8.178	1.259
1971:1	2.493	30.20	7.2	7.615	1.324
1971:2	3.602	31.25	7.0	7.718	1.385
1972:1	3.536	32.05	5.1	7.552	1.437
1972:2	3.098	33.25	7.5	7.663	1.476
1973:1	3.966	34.60	8.1	7.865	1.517
1973:2	4.686	36.90	13.3	8.495	1.552
1974:1	6.160	38.20	7.0	8.917	1.592
1974:2	5.318	39.95	9.2	9.220	1.676
1975:1	5.844	42.20	11.3	8.923	1.725
1975:2	6.707	43.45	5.9	8.980	1.779
1976:1	5.477	45.40	9.0	8.975	1.856
1976:2	5.699	47.55	9.5	9.035	1.922
1977:1	5.984	50.75	13.5	8.990	1.935
1977:2	6.913	54.00	12.8	9.137	1.993
1978:1	7.195	57.25	12.0	9.522	2.007
1978:2	7.479	61.95	16.4	10.067	2.029
1979:1	8.964	66.10	13.4	10.717	1.801
1979:2	8.757	70.10	12.1	1.783	1.748

a. Forecast of expected inflation, as described in text.
b. Price of constant quality house.
c. Growth rate of 2.
d. New home conventional mortgage rate.
e. Estimate of CPI index of maintenance, taxes, and insurance.

Whether or not this is all there is to it is not clear a priori. Again, people can "finance" a cash flow problem in all sorts of ways. Furthermore, the inflation and fixed payment mortgage mean that people accumulate real equity in a house faster than otherwise. This makes it easier for people to "trade up" sooner than otherwise. Since most people who buy a house have previously owned one, this effect could dominate the cash flow one, which is probably more an issue for first-time buyers.

There are really two issues. The first is whether the shadow price of the borrowing constraint is big enough to matter, and, second, whether it is an increasing function of the nominal interest. Since this constraint is not directly measurable, the first question is difficult to answer, but it is important. Suppose it is simply a constant. Then its addition is like raising the depreciation rate in our calculation. That will not affect the direction of changes in the interest cost index; but it will make the changes more stable in percentage terms, so that the change in the index and on the CPI will not be as great.

We have a simple test directed toward the second question. Equation (11) can be rewritten as

$$\frac{U_h/U_c}{q} = (1 - \theta)i - \pi + d \tag{11$'$}$$

Now this, of course, is not a demand curve. We can get one by incorporating it and other first order conditions and constraints. But if we know U_h/U_c, (11) would give us house price as a function of the real interest rate, and by entering the nominal rate as well, we could test to see which matters.

Let $\bar{R} = (U_h/U_c)p$. $\bar{R}$ is a measure of nominal imputed rent. Of course, it depends on all of the demographic, income, etc. variables that go into demand. Actual rents, R, paid by actual renters also reflect their marginal rates of substitution. $\bar{R}$ and R should be different numbers, but we might suppose that the two being based on similar tastes, income, and demographic parameters, move in the same direction. Assuming this to be the case, we fit equations of the form

$$R/p_h = R(((1 - \theta)i - \pi), i) \tag{25}$$

(where R is the CPI rent index and p_h the constant quality house price) to test to see which variable, the real or nominal interest rate, is significant in explaining real imputed rent. We should expect the real rate to have a positive coefficient and, if the cash flow variable is significant, i should also have a positive coefficient.

Again, we assumed that $\bar{R}$ moves like the CPI rent index. We normalized the index by assuming that the $\bar{R}$ for the constant quality new 1974 house used in our house price index was $4,000 per year in the second half of 1978. (Its price was $61,950.) Equation (25) was estimated using ordinary least squares. Since we do not expect house prices to adjust immediately, we estimated R/p_h as a function of lagged values (for two years) of real and nominal interest rates. Using our forecast of house price inflation and 25 percent tax rate, semiannual OLS estimates for the period 1968–1979 were

$$R/P_h = .078 + .225r + .211r_{-1} + .180r_{-2} + .187r_{-3} + .062r_{-4}$$
$$(2.93) \quad (2.21)^{-1} \quad (1.94)^{-2} \quad (2.21)^{-3} \quad (0.67)$$

$$- .299i + .266i_{-1} + .004i_{-2} + .236i_{-3} + .346i_{-4}$$
$$(-1.58) \quad (0.76) \quad (-0.01) \quad (0.70) \quad (-1.72)$$

$\bar{R}^2 = .96$ D.W. $= 1.78$
(t ratios in parentheses; lags are $\frac{1}{2}$ year)

Clearly, the effect of real rates has the right sign and is significant, and the effect of nominal rates is probably insignificant and has the wrong sign. We dropped nominal rates from the equation and estimated R/P_h as a function of present and past real rates.

The estimated equation was

$$R/p_h = .064 + .273r + .285r_{-1} + .153r_{-2} + .178r_{-3} + .115r_{-4}$$
$$(3.49) \quad (3.82) \quad (1.88) \quad (2.24) \quad (1.38)$$

$$(26)$$

$\bar{R}^2 = .95$ D.W. $= 1.04$
(t values in parentheses; lags are $\frac{1}{2}$ year)

Adjustments for serial correlations made no significant difference in the estimates.

If our theory is right and we have measured $\bar{R}$ properly, then the constant term in (26) should represent the depreciation rate, plus the shadow price of borrowing limits, plus other costs (e.g., maintenance and taxes) that might as a first approximation be taken to be proportional to house price. The equation suggests that the sum of these is about 6.4 percent per year. We should also expect the sum of the coefficients of the real rate to be unity. It turns out to be almost exactly unity.

That is a rather interesting result. It suggests not only that real rates matter, but also that imputed rents are discounted fully (since the coefficients sum to unity). Of course, that the sum of the coefficients adds to unity is a result of our earlier assumption about rents in 1978, but we should guess that $4,000 rental is sufficiently plausible that the results can be taken as a sensible first approximation.

We also used nominal interest rates as a proxy for expected inflation. In doing this we assumed the "gross" real rate to be constant. Estimating R/P_h (real imputed rent) as a function of lagged nominal rates this should (if inflation is unaffected by i) give us an "estimate" of the marginal tax rate. That is, the sum of the coefficients of the lagged i should be $-.25$. If the cash flow problem also matters the sum should exceed $-.25$.

Our OLS estimates using nominal mortgage rates was

$$R/P_h = .164 - .642i + .047i_{-1} - .189i_{-2} - .224i_{-3}$$
$$ (-2.73) \quad (0.10) \quad\quad (-0.42) \quad (-0.53)$$
$$+ .081i_{-4} - .003i_{-5} - .299i_{-6}$$
$$(0.19) \quad\quad (-0.01) \quad\quad (-1.14)$$

$$\bar{R}^2 = .92 \qquad D.W. = .43$$

Again, correcting for serial correlation did not affect the result.

The sum of the coefficients is close to $-.7$ which is not consistent with either hypothesis. Our guess as to what is happening is that the gross real rate has fallen, and it is inversely correlated with nominal rates, so that i is taking away some of the real rate's explanatory power. Since we cannot tell how much was taken away, we cannot conclude much from the results, other than that since i has a negative effect on the cash flow, the tilt problem cannot have been the major factor.

While these results are suggestive, they are not entirely satisfactory. Our equation (22) suggests that actual and imputed rents cannot be expected to move together, so that R may not be a good proxy for $\bar{R}$. A more satisfactory approach (along lines like those in Kearl [1979]) would be to set up a model of a housing market and estimate a reduced form equation for relative house prices. The model would give current relatives price as a function of things in the demand curve (e.g., r, i, and y) and current stock of housing.

Unfortunately, we do not have good data for the stock of housing for the period in which we are interested. We have instead estimated house prices as functions of current past values of demand and supply variables in the hope of estimating some dynamic process that determines both prices and housing stock.

We have experimented with several variants of reduced form equation, using various measures of income, both current and permanent, demographic variables like the number of households, and a measure of construction costs. Coefficients of these variables tended to be very sensitive to changes in specification (e.g., sometimes income had a negative effect) in a way that did not give us much confidence in the ability of the equations to explain house prices. In general, however, it is the case that even though other variables have not worked well, we consistently had the result that r has a negative and generally significant effect and i an insignificant (and frequently positive) effect on house prices.

Hence, while we are not (until we get a better grasp of supply side variables) able to produce satisfying price equations, we do have some weak evidence that it is real rather than nominal interest rates that affect people's behavior. This is in contrast with recent work by Kearl (1979) which finds a significant effect during the 1960–1971 period. At this point, we do not try to reconcile the differences. We suspect that it has something to do with the different periods used; but as Kearl's is a broader, more complicated model, it may be due to the ways the models are set up.

Conclusions

Standard price theory suggests that the appropriate measure of homeownership cost is significantly different from that used in the Consumer Price Index. Our estimates suggest that something on the order of a quarter of the price rise as measured by the CPI is spurious.

The thrust of the analysis is that money illusion in the tax system, allowing homeowners to deduct nominal interest but escape taxes on nominal capital gains, plus an inability of gross real rates to rise (they have probably fallen) generates the results. The tax subsidy to homeowners due to inflation is roughly their marginal tax rate times the inflation rate. Not only does this rise with inflation, but because it is proportional to tax bracket, it becomes increasingly inequitable as inflation increases. People in different brackets appear to have had significantly different inflation rates.

Finally, there is some preliminary evidence that households do, in fact, see through inflation illusions and discount future "rents" at the after-tax real rate.

REFERENCES

Boadway R., and N. Bruce. 1978. "The Effect of the Corporate Tax on Investment under Historic and Replacement Cost Depreciation." Discussion Paper No. 314, Queen's University, Canada.

Carlson, John. 1977. "Short Term Interest Rates as Predictors of Inflation: Comment." *American Economic Review.* (June) p. 471.

de Leeuw, F., and L. Ozanne. 1979. "Investment in Housing and Federal Income Tax." Presented at Brookings Conference on Taxation. October.

Diamond, Douglas. 1979. "Taxes, Inflation, Speculation and the Cost of Homeownership: 1963–1978." Presented at Meetings of American Real Estate and Urban Economics Association (AREUEA). Washington, D.C., May.

Feldstein, M.; J. Green; and E. Sheshinski. 1978. "Inflation and Taxes in a Growing Economy." *Journal of Political Economy* 86: 552–570.

Friedan, B., and A. Solomon. 1977. *The Nation's Housing Needs.* Joint Center for Urban Studies, Cambridge, Massachusetts.

Hendershott, P., and S. Hu. 1979. "Inflation, Taxes, the Mortgage Contract and Benefits to Housing." Presented at AREUEA Meetings. May.

Kearl, J. 1978. "Inflation and Relative Price Distortions: The Case of Housing." *Review of Economics and Statistics.* pp. 609–614.

_____. 1979. "Inflation, Mortgages and Housing." *Journal of Political Economy* 87: 1115–38.

Swan, C. 1978. "The Affordability of Unaffordable Housing." Prepared for Housing Cost Task Force. February.

Van Order, R., and K. Villani. 1979. "Alternative Measures of Housing Costs." Presented at AREUEA Meetings, Atlanta. December.

Villani, K. 1979. "The Tax Subsidy to Housing in an Inflationary Environment." HUD Working Paper.

Weicher, J. 1979. "The Affordability of New Homes." *AREUEA Journal.* Summer.

9

EXPANDING AND IMPROVING THE CPI RENT COMPONENT

Larry Ozanne

Rapid inflation has greatly increased the importance of measuring housing cost changes accurately. From 1967 to January 1981 the Consumer Price Index (CPI) showed rents rising 201 percent and homeownership costs rising 336 percent compared to a 248 percent rise in other prices. The CPI's homeownership cost component has already received considerable attention because of its much faster rise than other prices. Now, the rent component is gaining increased attention because it has risen less rapidly than other prices and because a rent index representative of owner-occupied housing is being considered as a replacement for the present homeownership component.

Our initial research on the CPI rent component at The Urban Institute has already yielded interesting insights about housing cost inflation and has found a source that promises more. We have tentatively estimated that the CPI rent component underestimates rent inflation by 0.6 to 0.7 percent yearly because of unmeasured depreciation. Adding this increment to the rent component over the 1967 to 1981 period would raise it to 219, closing over a third of the gap between the rent component and all nonhousing items. We recommend that an improved depreciation estimate be made and incorporated in the CPI rent component.

[The author is senior research associate, The Urban Institute.]

We have also constructed a preliminary replacement for the CPI's homeownership cost component. Our replacement is a rent index of rented single-family homes. While not weighted to fully reflect the owner-occupied stock, it is close enough to identify the major outlines of indexes that eventually could be incorporated in the CPI. Our rent index for single-family dwellings rose only 0.4 percent per year less than an index for all rental dwellings. This suggests that the current CPI rent component is an adequate proxy for what a new homeownership index would show. The approximation is even better than it first appears because this 0.4 percent overestimate by the present rent index offsets part of the 0.6 to 0.7 percent underestimate from unmeasured depreciation. The bottom line, in our opinion, is that the present difference between the CPI's homeownership cost component and its rent component is a good estimate of how the measurement of inflation in homeownership will change if a rent-based index is substituted.

The other main insight from our research to date is that the Annual Housing Survey (AHS) provides a promising source for extending the CPI rent component to additional places and for improving the index as it is currently constructed.

Next, I briefly describe the current index, discuss ways in which the CPI can be improved and expanded, and then describe the AHS. In the following sections, I report on two studies of the CPI rent component and recommend areas for further study.

The Issues

THE CPI RENT COMPONENT

The CPI rent component is available for the whole of metropolitan and urban areas, for 28 individual metropolitan areas, and for 20 region- and city-size categories.[1] The index measures the change in rent for a representative sample of rental dwellings. Rents for sample dwellings are obtained in successive months and the ratio of total rent for all dwellings in the latter month relative to the former month measures rental price changes.[2] To insure that these rent changes reflect price changes for constant quality housing, a check is made that the utilities and structural services provided in rent have not changed. When changes occur in the utilities included in rent, the affected rents are adjusted to net out the change. When structural changes occur, the affected rents are excluded from the index.

ISSUES

From 1967 through January 1981 the Consumer Price Index (CPI) component for homeownership costs has risen 336 percent and the residential rent component has risen 201 percent.[3] These rapid increases—and the disparity between them—have created much interest in the way the CPI measures housing cost changes. Considerable attention has already been focused on the homeownership component.[4] Attention to the homeownership index has stirred interest in the rent component because a rent index is being considered as an alternative to the present homeownership component. Interest in the rent component has also risen because that index shows rents inflating less rapidly than average prices for consumer goods or for the inputs used to provide rental housing.

The heightened interest in measuring rent inflation makes the present a good time to consider ways in which the CPI rent component can be improved and extended. One needed extension is a separate index for rental units that resemble owner-occupied housing. Such an index is the major alternative under consideration by the Bureau of Labor Statistics for replacing the current homeownership component.

It is also important to extend the rent index to as many geographic areas as possible. Rental markets are localized so rent inflation can vary substantially among areas. Rental markets are localized because dwellings are durable and cannot be moved, and because neighborhood boundaries are strong and slow to change. These factors permit rents to inflate faster in one area than in another. Many other goods, like cars or television sets, are easily transported to higher priced areas and shoppers are less sensitive to neighborhood boundaries when making such purchases. Thus extensive geographic measurement of price changes is more important for housing than for most other goods and services.

Shortcomings in the procedures for constructing the rent index also merit evaluation and repair. The present rent index probably understates price increases for constant quality housing. Dwellings gradually depreciate so that the CPI's successive observations on a dwelling's rent reflect both price increases and quality decreases. The downward effect on rents from the quality decrease causes the understatement in the CPI. The magnitude of this bias should be measured and adjustments made to the present index. In this paper I present evidence about the magnitude of this understatement.

The present index measures contract rent which is an irregular combination of rents that include all utilities, rents that include some, and rents that include none. This irregularity distorts comparisons of rent indexes among areas because the fraction of units including utilities differs. Almost four-fifths of the rental units in the New York metropolitan area include heat in rent while less than one-fifth do in St. Louis. Comparability could be achieved through a gross rent index or separate indexes for each utility included. A useful analytic improvement would be to separate gross rent inflation into a structural and a utilities component.

THE ANNUAL HOUSING SURVEY

The opportunity for expanding and improving the CPI rent index is greatly enhanced by the Annual Housing Survey (AHS). Since 1974 the survey has been following panels of dwellings about which it collects detailed dwelling and occupant information. One panel represents the nation and 60 other panels represent 60 large metropolitan areas. The national panel contains about 70,000 dwellings that are surveyed in the last quarter of each year. Each metropolitan panel contains 5 or 15 thousand units that are surveyed in 12 monthly subpanels from April of one year through March of the next. Each metropolitan survey is repeated every three to four years and the 60 surveys are staggered with 15 to 20 areas being surveyed per year. Rental units comprise about 35 percent of the national sample and varying portions of the metropolitan areas. The national panel identifies dwellings as located within 125 metropolitan areas and within 32 region and size-of-place categories. Forty-seven metropolitan panels identify central city or suburban location and, where suburban counties are large enough, they are separately identified.

All Annual Housing Surveys collect the same basic dwelling and occupant characteristics.[5] Rents are recorded as are the utilities included. The cost of utilities paid directly by the household is also requested.

Analyses of the CPI

At The Urban Institute Thomas Thibodeau, Stephen Malpezzi, and I have completed two AHS-based analyses of the CPI rent index. In these analyses we have shown that the current CPI rent index is a good proxy for a rent index replacement of homeownership costs. That is, a rent index for a sample of rental units representing the owner-occupied stock would move similarly to the present index. We have also estimated that the downward bias in the CPI rent index component from unmeasured depreciation is 0.6 to 0.7 percent per year. In the process of reaching these conclusions we established that procedures similar to those used to construct the CPI can be applied in the AHS and will yield rent indexes similar to the CPI's. This means the AHS can be useful for extending rent indexes to areas covered only by the AHS and for evaluating the CPI.

ANALYSIS OF THE NATIONAL ANNUAL HOUSING SURVEY

Our finding about a rent index replacement for the CPI homeownership component comes from a study that tried to replicate the CPI rent index with the AHS.[6] The first step was to document CPI procedures and assess how well they could be replicated with the AHS. Sample designs, questionnaire contents, and formulae for computing the index were examined. We found that the basic CPI procedures could be applied to the AHS in spite of numerous technical differences.

The second step was to construct CPI-type indexes using the AHS and check the results against the CPI. We constructed rent indexes from the 1974 through 1977 years of the national AHS. During this time the CPI index was published for 23 metropolitan areas individually and for all metropolitan areas and urban places together. We constructed AHS indexes for the same places.

Table 1 compares our indexes to the CPI rent component. The bottom line of the table shows that over a three-year period quantitative differences between the indexes are minor. From 1974 to 1977 the CPI component for all metropolitan areas and urban places rose 18.3 percent while the AHS analog rose 19.3 percent. The average of the CPI indexes for 23 metropolitan areas rose 19.4 percent over the same period while the average of the AHS indexes rose 19.9 percent. Because the two indexes are so

TABLE 1

CPI RENT COMPONENT AND ITS AHS ANALOG
(Percentage Changes)

YEARS (DEC. TO DEC.)	ALL METRO AND URBAN PLACES			23 METRO AREAS		
	CPI	AHS	Difference	CPI	AHS	Difference
1974–75	5.32	5.79	.47	5.30	6.10	.80
1975–76	5.48	5.24	−.24	5.91	5.22	−.69
1976–77	6.47	7.16	.69	7.07	7.36	.29
1974–77	18.28	19.30	1.02	19.41	19.86	.45

SOURCE: Thibodeau and Ozanne [1981], pp. 35 and 39.

close, we conclude that the AHS is a suitable source for extending and analyzing the CPI rent component.

Once the CPI analogs were constructed it was simple to calculate rent indexes for single-family rental units. Comparison of a rent index for single-family housing to that for all rental housing should indicate whether a rent index replacement for the CPI homeownership component would differ much from the present CPI rent index.

Table 2 presents a national rent index for all rental units and separate indexes for single-family and multifamily units.[7] The single-family index is lower than the aggregate index in each of the three years but the two indexes never differ by as much as half a percentage point. The cumulative differences over three years is only about one percentage point out of a 19-point increase. The closeness of the two indexes convinces me that any rent index proxy for homeownership costs will closely approximate the current CPI rent index. It will therefore be substantially below the current homeownership cost index.

Even though a rent index for homeowners will be close to that for all rental units, a rental sample more closely resembling owner-occupied dwellings should be constructed. Homeowners make up almost two-thirds of all households so that even small differences can be important in the total CPI.

Besides national indexes by structure type, we constructed separate indexes for many metropolitan areas not reported by the CPI. The current CPI sample and the national AHS both contain about 20,000 rental dwellings, but the CPI sample is concentrated in 85 metropolitan areas and urban places while the AHS is spread among 461 metropolitan areas and county groups. As a result the AHS can identify more areas but has a

TABLE 2

NATIONAL AHS RENT INDEXES BY STRUCTURE TYPE
(Percentage Changes)

Years (Dec. to Dec.)	All	Single-Family	Multifamily
1974–75	5.78	5.23	5.93
1975–76	5.23	5.10	5.28
1976–77	7.09	6.63	7.26
1974–77	19.20	18.03	19.62

SOURCE: Thibodeau and Ozanne [1981], p. 35.

smaller sample size in each area. The 28 places identified by the CPI since 1978 have samples of 390 or more while only 3 areas in the AHS have that many units. On the other hand the AHS identifies 125 metropolitan areas and 50 of these have 30 or more observations. Thus, indexes for more places can be computed with the AHS but most of them will have greater sample variance than the CPI indexes.

We have computed indexes for all 125 identified metropolitan areas in the national AHS. An important next step is to estimate variances for these indexes so that users can judge the indexes' reliability. Another important step would be to construct CPI-type indexes from the metropolitan Annual Housing Surveys. This would provide 32 more metropolitan indexes than the CPI currently reports. Furthermore, the 60 metropolitan surveys provide samples twice as large as those currently used by the CPI for the 28 areas it reports. The larger sample sizes could be used to construct indexes for submarkets such as central cities and suburban areas. These indexes would have to span three or four years because the metropolitan surveys follow three- or four-year cycles. If annual indexes were needed, the national AHS could be used to infer rental changes for intervening years. The surveys become available one to two years after they are administered.

ANALYSIS OF THE METROPOLITAN AHS

In a separate study we estimated linear equations to explain rent in terms of dwelling characteristics and services provided.[8] These "hedonic" equations provide an alternative means for calculating rent indexes that is useful for analyzing shortcomings of the CPI procedure. We used hedonic methods to infer separate indexes for structural services and heat costs included in rent. Here I use our hedonic equations to infer the depreciation bias in the CPI.

The Hedonic Equations We estimated 59 hedonic rent equations, one for each metropolitan area with an available AHS data tape.[9] At the time the work was undertaken, no area had surveys for separate years.[10] Consequently, all our information about rent changes was derived from survey data spanning a single year. Recall that each survey was administered in 12 monthly installments with each installment being a probability sample of the entire metropolitan area. We used each hedonic equation to measure rental price changes between months. The 12 months included in an AHS survey run from April of one year through March of the next. We used surveys beginning in April of 1974, 1975, and 1976.

Our hedonic equation has the form

$$\ln R = aX + bTIME + cTIME \cdot HEAT + d_1 AGE + d_2 AGE^2 + e \quad (1)$$

where

$\ln R$ is the natural logarithm of contract rent;

X is a vector of dwelling characteristics;

TIME is the month in which a dwelling is interviewed—0 for April, 1 for May, and so on to 11 for March;

HEAT is an indicator for heat included in rent—it is unity if a dwelling's rent includes heat, zero if it does not;

AGE is the age in years of the building—it enters linearly and squared;

$a-d_2$ are coefficients giving the contribution of their respective variables to rent—b, c, d_1 and d_2 are interpreted below;

e is unexplained determinants of rent—assumed random.

We interpret the coefficients b and c as rates of rental price change and the coefficients d_1 and d_2 as determinants of the depreciation rate. Our interpretation of d_1 and d_2 is explained below. First, I examine the meaning and the estimates of b and c. (All coefficients were estimated by regression analysis.)

Differentiating the hedonic equation with respect to TIME gives

$$\frac{dR/R}{dTIME} \begin{cases} = b & \text{if HEAT} = 0 \\ = b + c & \text{if HEAT} = 1 \end{cases}$$

The differential says that rent changes 100b percent per month for dwellings without heat included and 100 (b + c) percent per month for dwellings with heat included. Because these are differentials, they give the change in rent per month holding other characteristics of the dwelling constant. (The other characteristics are given by X and AGE.) This is why we interpret b and b + c as price indexes.

Additionally, one can assume that b gives a rent index for structural services that applies to all dwellings and that c gives an index for heat costs included in rent.

We expected our regression estimates of b and b + c to be positive for the 1974 through 1976 survey years because of the general inflation over the period. Furthermore, if one assumes rents for structural services rose similarly for dwellings with and without heat included in rent, then one would expect c to be positive as well because costs for heating were rising more rapidly than rents.[11]

Our estimates of b are statistically greater than zero in 37 out of 59 areas and are never significantly less than zero. The median estimate is b = .005 which compounds to a 6 percent annual rate. Only a few estimates were unreasonably high, e.g., Buffalo's b compounds to an 18 percent annual rate.

The majority of our estimates of c were close to zero. Thirty-five were not statistically different from zero and of the remainder 8 were positive and 6 were actually negative. Thus rents which included heat typically rose at the same rate as those which excluded heat. Since landlords' costs for heating fuels rose faster than contract rents, it seems likely that rents for structural services rose less rapidly for dwellings which included utilities than in dwellings which did not. Further investigation of the effects of rising utility costs on rent are needed.

We interpret the coefficients d_1 and d_2 as determinants of the depreciation rate for rental housing. Differentiating the hedonic equation with respect to AGE while holding constant other characteristics gives

$$\frac{dR/R}{dAGE} = d_1 + 2d_2 AGE$$

This says rent changes by $100(d_1 + 2d_2 AGE)$ percent for each additional year of age a building has. Buildings generally depreciate as they age so we expect d_1 to be negative and d_2 to be positive or negative depending on whether the depreciation rate decreases or increases with age, respectively. The medians of our 59 estimates are $d_1 = -.007$ and $d_2 = 0$. Thus the estimates imply rental dwellings typically depreciate $7/10$ of a percent yearly throughout their lives.

Estimating Bias in the CPI   The hedonic equations can be used to estimate the depreciation bias in the CPI rent component. The CPI measures rental price changes from the rent of dwellings at two points in time. If the dwellings are gradually depreciating, then rent changes will understate the rent change for a constant quality dwelling. Our hedonic depreciation estimate says that understatement is typically $7/10$ of a percent per year.

Our hedonic estimates of rental price changes provide a second estimate of the understatement. The hedonic coefficients b and c refer to rent changes for dwellings of constant quality and age, so indexes constructed from them will be free of the CPI's aging bias. The difference between hedonic and CPI rent indexes, therefore, gives a second estimate of the CPI depreciation bias.

I have constructed rent indexes from our b and c coefficients for the 23 metropolitan areas with CPI indexes in the 1974 through 1977 years.[12] Because the CPI refers to contract rent I constructed a weighted average of the rate for units without and with heat. The weights reflect the proportion of units including heat in rent.

Table 3 shows the hedonic index, the CPI index, and the difference between the two. The hedonic index is usually greater than the CPI index as

TABLE 3

HEDONIC AND CPI ESTIMATES OF ANNUAL PERCENTAGE RENT CHANGE

Place	(1) Hedonic	(2) CPI	(3) Difference (1)-(2)
April 1974 to April 1975			
Boston	11.3	5.0	6.3
Dallas*	4.3	4.2	.1
Detroit	4.6	4.9	−.3
Los Angeles+	7.5	5.2	2.3
Minneapolis	4.4	4.0	.4
Pittsburgh	4.7	4.1	.6
Washington*	6.4	6.7	−.3
April 1975 to April 1976			
Atlanta+	8.9	1.9	7.0
Chicago+	4.3	3.9	.4
Cincinnati+	8.5	3.5	5.0
Kansas City+	4.8	3.6	1.2
Milwaukee*	5.9	5.4	.5
Philadelphia+	12.4	6.2	6.2
San Diego*	10.4	6.7	3.7
San Francisco+	8.5	5.2	3.3
Arpil 1976 to April 1977			
Baltimore+	7.1	6.6	.5
Buffalo*	14.1	5.2	8.9
Cleveland*	6.8	6.6	.2
Honolulu+	0.4	4.0	−3.6
Houston	13.9	13.1	.8
New York	7.8	5.1	2.7
Seattle*	5.3	8.6	−3.3
St. Louis	5.1	5.1	0
Median			.6

*Year is from March to March.
+Year is from May to May.

it should be if there is a depreciation bias in the CPI index. The hedonic index is greater than the CPI index 18 out of 23 times. Furthermore, the median difference between the indexes is $^6/_{10}$ of a percent which lies close to our median depreciation rate of $^7/_{10}$ of a percent. Thus, the hedonic rent index and the hedonic depreciation estimate imply that the CPI rent index is downward biased by about 0.6 to 0.7 percent a year because of unmeasured depreciation.

Differences between the hedonic and the CPI indexes on table 3 are sometimes quite large. I think the large discrepancies arise because of random rent variation within the AHS survey year. The 12 monthly panels represented in each survey year are small enough that random fluctuations in rent from one month to the next can be large relative to the true monthly rent inflation. The hedonic rent indexes could be improved by constructing them between AHS waves rather than within them. Sample sizes in each survey year would be large enough to cancel most random rent fluctuations and the true rent change over the three to four years between surveys would be much larger than within a single year. An added benefit is that the hedonic indexes could be compared to CPI-type indexes constructed from the AHS data. Using just AHS data avoids random variation between the AHS and CPI samples and any tendency for households to respond differently to the two surveys.

Next Steps

At several points in my discussion I have identified subjects needing further study. In this final section I give a complete picture of where I think research on measuring rent inflation should be headed.

The following four tasks seem important to me:

- Extending the CPI rent component to additional areas
- Constructing indexes which treat utilities comparabably among areas
- Improving our estimates of the depreciation bias in the CPI
- Improving our rent index replacement for the CPI homeownership component

None of the subjects seems to me unambiguously more important than the others. They are listed in the above order to facilitate their presentation.

EXTENDING THE CPI RENT COMPONENT TO ADDITIONAL AREAS

Since rents are set in local markets, it would be useful to extend rent in-dexes to additional areas. The AHS makes it inexpensive to do so. The repeating metropolitan surveys allow CPI-type indexes to be extended from the present 28 areas to 60. Furthermore, separate indexes by central city-suburban location and by structure type can be explored. The large sample sizes of the metropolitan AHS ensure that these extensions of the CPI will be measured at least as precisely as the current CPI indexes. Of course they will not be available monthy, as is the CPI.

The national AHS can be used to fill in the three or four intervening years between metropolitan surveys for the 60 large metropolitan areas in-cluded in both panels. It can also provide some information on rent changes in another 65 small metropolitan areas and rural areas. Cur-rently, rural areas are not represented at all in the CPI. Use of metropoli-tan indexes from the national AHS should be coupled with estimates of their sample variance because sample sizes are small in most metropolitan areas.

CONSTRUCTING INDEXES TREATING UTILITIES COMPARABLY AMONG AREAS

Only indexes that include the same utilities (and other kinds of services) can be meaningfully compared among areas. When the AHS is used to ex-tend the CPI to additional areas it would be simple to also construct com-parable indexes. Either a single gross rent index or separate indexes with common sets of included utilities could be constructed.

Besides treating utilities consistently in rent, it would be useful to analyze the impact of utility cost increases on rents. Our first analysis found rents with utilities rising no more rapidly than those without. Does this finding hold up with better estimates obtained from repeating surveys of the AHS? If so, what does it imply for the rate of rent increases for structural services in units with and without utilities included in rent?

Comparable rent indexes will probably continue to show the substantial variation in rent inflation among areas that the present CPI shows. If so, analysis of supply and demand factors explaining these differences could be pursued.

IMPROVING ESTIMATES OF DEPRECIATION BIAS IN CPI

Our first estimates of the depreciation bias in the CPI rent index center around 0.6 to 0.7 percent per year. However, several hedonic rent indexes yielded much larger or smaller estimates. In the preceding chapter I pointed out that our estimates could be substantially improved by use of the AHS's repeat surveys in metropolitan areas. Use of repeat surveys would reduce random errors in the hedonic rent indexes relative to the size of actual rent inflation. Their use would also remove sampling variability from the comparison between hedonic and CPI indexes because CPI-analogs could be constructed from the AHS.

IMPROVING OUR RENT INDEX REPLACEMENT FOR THE CPI HOMEOWNERSHIP COMPONENT

We constructed a rent index for single-family dwellings to determine whether a rent index replacement for homeownership costs would differ from the current CPI rent index. We found that a single-family index would not differ much. The next step is to select a sample of rental dwellings which represents the owner-occupied stock as closely as possible in terms of dwelling size, structure type, location, etc. Our basic finding is unlikely to change, but even small changes in inflation rates are important when so many persons are affected.

REFERENCES

Dougherty, Ann, and Robert Van Order. "Inflation and Housing Costs." In *House Prices and Inflation*. John A. Tuccillo and Kevin E. Villani, eds. Washington, D.C.: The Urban Institute Press, 1981.

Malpezzi, Stephen; Larry Ozanne; and Thomas Thibodeau. 1980. "Characteristic Prices of Housing in Fifty-Nine Metropolitan Areas." Contract Report 1367-1. The Urban Institute, Washington, D.C.

Thibodeau, Thomas, and Larry Ozanne. 1981. "Constructing a Rent Index from the Annual Housing Survey," Contract Report 1443. The Urban Institute, Washington, D.C.

U.S. Bureau of the Census. 1976. Current Housing Reports, Series H-170-74-5, Detroit Michigan SMSA, Annual Housing Survey: 1974, *Housing Characteristics for Selected Metropolitan Areas*. U.S. Government Printing Office, Washington, D.C.

U.S. Bureau of Labor Statistics. 1981. *CPI Detailed Reports, January 1981*. U.S. Government Printing Office, Washington, D.C., March.

10

MEASURING THE COST OF SHELTER FOR HOMEOWNERS

Robert Gillingham, John S. Greenlees, and William S. Reece

Recent economic developments have stirred a renewed interest in the development and implementation of improved measures of the cost of shelter for homeowners. Having devoted considerable attention to this issue over the past eight years, the Bureau of Labor Statistics (BLS) shares this interest. Since 1972 the BLS has raised a series of conceptual and operational questions concerning the treatment of owner-occupied housing in the Consumer Price Index (CPI), attempting to stir debate and reach a sufficient consensus to introduce improved procedures into the index. Although such a consensus has yet to be reached, the bureau maintains its interest in this area and is currently engaged in a project to estimate several alternative shelter cost indexes in order to evaluate their relative merits as a possible replacement for the current approach. This summary will describe the background and conceptual framework out of which this project has developed, outline the major objectives of the project, describe the data bases, and discuss several statistical issues which must be addressed.

[Robert Gillingham is chief, Division of Price and Index Number Research, Bureau of Labor Statistics, and John S. Greenlees and William S. Reece are economists, Bureau of Labor Statistics.]

Background

For the past eight years, the BLS has been evaluating alternative methods of measuring the costs of owner-occupied housing in the CPI. In preparation for the recently completed revision of the index, bureau staff proposed that the shelter component of the CPI—for both renters and owners—measure the cost of consuming the flow of shelter services provided by a housing unit. This approach, which is comparable to that incorporated in the national accounts, focuses on consumption and abstracts from the investment aspects of home purchase decisions. The BLS proposal to implement the flow of services approach in the CPI initiated a long discussion among academic, business, and labor groups interested in the compilation and use of the CPI. A series of position papers on the issue[1] was prepared by the BLS. As these papers indicate, although the bureau staff initially favored the adoption of a rental equivalence approach to measuring shelter costs, alternatives which focused on the components of user cost were also given substantial consideration in an attempt to find an alternative which could achieve the support necessary to justify implementation. The only consensus which could be achieved, however, was that further research on the flow of services alternatives should be conducted before a major change is made in the CPI.

Given this decision the bureau is currently working on the development of experimental shelter services indexes. It is interesting to note that not only have current economic conditions renewed interest in the housing component of the CPI, but recent trends in the housing components of the index have led interested parties to raise some of the same questions which were raised by BLS staff during recent years. Recent trends have given an increased empirical content to what had been primarily a conceptual debate. I hope the current environment can contribute to the development and acceptance of an improved housing component for the CPI.

Conceptual Framework

Gilligham (1980) outlines the conceptual issues which the research staff of the BLS views as most important in developing a shelter services cost index. This paper compares the rental equivalence and user cost alternatives to measuring shelter cost, concluding that the rental equivalence approach is the more promising. To summarize briefly, if we start by considering a taxless, perfectly competitive, frictionless world without uncertainty it can be shown that the user cost of a housing unit in period t is

$$C_t = r_t P_t - A_t + Z_t \tag{1}$$

where r is the (single) rate of interest, P is the average price of the housing unit in the period, A is the change in the price of the house over the period, and Z represents all other cost components. In equilibrium, the rental price of the housing unit, R, will be equal to the user cost, and, since we have assumed away frictions, the rent received by a landlord will be equal to the rent paid by a tenant. Thus, in a perfect world the following obtains

$$R_t^L = C_t = R_t^T \tag{2}$$

where the superscripts L and T denote landlord and tenant, respectively.

In a perfect world, then, measurement of the value of the flow of services from a housing unit is relatively trivial, and the choice between the user cost and rental equivalence approaches is essentially arbitrary. The difficulties arise when we drop the assumption of perfect certainty, thereby allowing for a structure of differing asset yields, and admit frictions, thereby allowing R^L to be less than R^T. Under these conditions, the user cost becomes

$$C_t = r_{e_t} E_t + r_{m_t} M_t - A_t + Z_t \tag{3}$$

where M and E are mortgage and equity amounts which sum to P, r_m is the mortgage interest rate and r_e is the opportunity cost of equity capital. The relationship between user cost, defined in this manner, and the alternative rent measures is now ambiguous and depends critically on the manner in which r_e is defined.

In Gillingham (1980) it is argued that the rent measures form bounds on admissable user cost measures and that, in general, a user cost measure will be certain to fall within these bounds if and only if r_e is defined as an internal rate of return on housing. That is, the household's user cost of owner-occupied housing or cost of consuming the flow of services from its housing unit must be at least as great as the income which the household could receive by renting the unit to someone else. This cost is independent of the capital gains achievable from holding housing assets, except insofar as such gains are reflected in rent levels. Each household determines its housing stock based on decisions regarding the expected rates of return on housing equity and other assets with varying characteristics. This determination is separate, however, from the decision as to the rate of consumption of housing services.[2] Such factors as the rate of change in house prices determine the rate of return on equity, but *ex post* capital gains do not affect the user cost. In the same way, defining r_e other than as the internal rate of return has the effect of incorrectly including in C some element of the investment return on housing investments. This result implies that rental equivalence measures are a necessary input into the development of acceptable user cost measures. This conclusion, combined with the volatility (demonstrated in Gillingham [1980]) of user cost measures which incorporate alternative measures of r_e, will be used to structure our current research project. First, we intend to focus on the development of rental equivalence measures as the conceptually preferred approach measuring the cost of shelter services. Second, despite this conclusion, we will still focus on obtaining improved measure of the components of user cost. Such measures will be of value for two reasons. First, if it is impossible to obtain an acceptable rental equivalence measure, at least some of the components of user cost can be used to obtain a modified measure of housing cost which might replace the current index. Second, the components of user cost can be combined with rental equivalence measures to obtain estimates of r_e—a worthwhile objective in its own right.

Before going on to describe the specifics of the research we are undertaking, it is important to digress to discuss a number of corollary conceptual issues which might potentially be the source of some confusion.

Friction Costs   The analysis in Gillingham (1980) allows for friction costs, but elaboration is warranted. The importance of frictions depends on the time period over which costs are measured. In the extremely short run, frictional costs are likely to swamp the other components of user cost. Only when frictions are either ignored or amortized over a sufficiently long period will their relative importance be small enough so that a shelter cost index will represent the more interesting long-term trends in the other cost components.

Taxes   Although Gillingham (1980) ignores taxes, it would be quite straightforward to build taxes into the analysis and obtain "before-tax" and "after-tax" prices. It should be recognized, however, that the treatment of taxes in the CPI is a separate issue relating to many components—e.g., medical care, sales taxes, etc. Although after-tax prices are clearly of more interest in explaining demand behavior, the appropriate treatment of taxes in the CPI is less straightforward. A user of an index such as the CPI must be careful to insure that the income and price measures used to evaluate welfare changes are comparable in terms of the taxes which they include.

Cost versus Marginal Price Measures   In constructing a CPI, it is appropriate to measure the total cost of a consumption flow, while for demand analysis a marginal price is appropriate. This issue relates not only to housing, where varying marginal tax rates make the budget constraint nonlinear, but also to a number of other goods such as electricity, water and natural gas. (Strictly speaking, the problem can apply to all goods subject to a sales tax.)

Ex post versus ex ante Prices   A similar problem arises in choosing between ex ante and ex post prices. For demand analysis, ex ante prices are presumably relevant. In constructing a CPI design to measure changes in actual costs, ex post costs are appropriate.

Outline of Current Projects

Current BLS research on improved measures of homeowner shelter costs can be divided into two concurrent efforts: the development of a rental equivalence index and the refinement of individual user cost component indexes. In addition, BLS personnel have undertaken two closely related research projects: an econometric study of the demand for housing services, and an analysis of past trends in the rate of return to investments in housing. These projects are now described briefly.

Development of a Rental Equivalence Index of Shelter Costs for Homeowners   The basic objective is to evaluate methodologies for estimating movements in the rental values of owner-occupied housing. This will involve an examination of the determinants of rent levels and rent changes, and identification of the relationship between the factors determining rent changes and the differential characteristics of renter- and owner-occupied units.

Data for this research will come primarily from the CPI rent index data base. The sample of rental units used in the CPI was significantly modified prior to the 1977 index revision; however, both the "old" and "new" samples provide between 60,000 to 80,000 rent quotations per year on a wide spectrum of rental units, including single-family homes. These files can also be merged with tract-level census information. This will make possible a multiple regression analysis of rent determination using housing-unit specific and neighborhood-specific "quality" measures.

The present CPI rent index is computed as a weighted average of the changes in rent levels in the sample. The first step in our analysis will be an historical simulation of this method, with the sample weights adjusted to represent the universe of owner-occupied rather than renter-occupied housing units. The general characteristics of these units will be obtained by comparing owner and tenant records in the BLS' 1972–1973 Consumer Expenditure Survey (CES).[3]

We next plan to estimate a series of hedonic regressions using the CPI rent samples. Both rent levels and rent changes will be used as dependent variables. The large number of potential explanatory variables and the broad locational distribution of the sample will enable us to identify which housing characteristics have been most closely associated with the rate of increase in rents. Further, the regression approach should make possible an evaluation of several potential empirical problems with rental and rental equivalence indexes. Among these problems are aging bias (measured rent change in any period presumably includes some correction for the increased age of the sample units) and attrition bias (there is a loss of some rental units from the sample each period, for example through conversion to condominium status).[4]

Improved User Cost Component Indexes   This phase of research will be useful both as an input to possible refinements in the present CPI methodology, and as part of an examination of historical movements in individual cost items—home purchase prices, mortgage interest, depreciation or appreciation, and repairs and maintenance expenditures.[5] Historical simulations will be generated under alternative definitional assumptions; we expect that these will further highlight the empirical volatility of user cost indexes which was referred to above.

Possibly the most important input to user cost calculations, and the one which has thus far received the most attention, is the Home Purchasing Price Index series. Home Purchase currently has a weight of approximately 10 percent in the CPI and is computed based on movements in prices of FHA-insured houses. Our research has utilized the FHA's 1969–1978 master statistical files, as well as the monthly CPI data tapes which are available through the present date. This data base comprises approximately two million FHA appraisal records, each containing a large amount of descriptive and locational information. Census tract-level data can also be merged with these house records for analytical purposes.

Research on the Home Purchase Index has had three broad objectives. First has been the use of hedonic regression analysis to determine the importance of accounting for intertemporal quality change in factors other than age and square footage, the only two quality measures currently included in the CPI methodology. Second has been an evaluation of techniques which correct for "truncation" of the FHA sample caused by the program's ceiling on the value of an insurable mortgage. Third, methods are being examined which address the problem of sample maldistribution. Because FHA's share of the housing market varies widely from city to city, the CPI's house price sample is highly skewed with respect to location, some large cities being severely underrepresented.

Some of the initial analytical results of this research are discussed in Greenlees (1981a, 1981b). Simulations of several alternative Home Purchase Indexes are presented at the local, regional, and national levels. The simulations indicate that the traditional BLS practice of "linking out" changes in the FHA mortgage ceiling has had a serious downward impact on the published CPI index. Thus, any improvement in the current index method, either through a hedonic or more traditional approach, should include a more appropriate adjustment for ceiling levels and changes. Meanwhile, our study of the FHA data is continuing, with comparisons of FHA indexes to alternative published series (Greenlees, 1981a) and the addition of more sophisticated econometric methods for analyzing truncated samples (Greenlees, 1981b).

Estimating a Demand Function for Housing Services   One key aspect of this study, which employs cross-section data from the 1972–1973 CES, is its conceptually equivalent treatment of owner and renter households. For owners, the measure of housing consumption is based on the estimated monthly rental value of the housing unit. The price of housing services is measured using the local rent index from the BLS's Family Budgets series, adjusted by the household's estimated marginal tax rate (since owner-occupants' implicit rental income is not taxed). Given these definitions, the study becomes, in part, an application of the rental equivalence framework, and the empirical results obtained thus far (see Gillingham and Hagemann, 1980) indicate that the model performs well.

Estimating the Rate of Return on Housing Investment   The first two research projects described will generate historical series of rental equivalence and user cost component indexes. These series will then be used to obtain estimates of the internal rate of return on housing investments. Specificially equation (3) above can be rewritten as

$$r_{e_t} = (C_t - r_{m_t}M_t + A_t - Z_t)/E_t \tag{4}$$

Using a rental equivalence index as the measures of C_t, the user cost of housing services, this equation can be solved to yield a historical series for r_{e_t}. This r_{e_t} can then be viewed as the appropriate variable influencing total investment in housing.

REFERENCES

Gillingham, Robert F. 1972. "Measurement in the Consumer Price Index of the Cost of Shelter for Homeowners." U.S. Bureau of Labor Statistics. June. (Revised, December 1973).

———. 1980. "Estimating the User Cost of Owner-Occupied Housing." *Monthly Labor Review.* (February):31–35.

———., and Robert Hagemann. 1980. "Cross-Sectional Estimation of a Simultaneous Model of Tenure Choice and Housing Services Demand." U.S. Bureau of Labor Statistics. July.

Greenlees, John S. 1981a. "Alternative Indexes of Home Purchase Prices, 1973–1978." U.S. Bureau of Labor Statistics. February.

———. 1981b. "Sample Truncation in FHA Data: Implications for Home Purchase Indexes." U.S. Bureau of Labor Statistics. January.

Muth, Richard F. 1972. "On the Measurement of Shelter Costs for Homeowners in the Consumer Price Index." U.S. Bureau of Labor Statistics. August.

U.S. Bureau of Labor Statistics. 1973. "Option Paper on the Treatment of Housing Prices." October.

———. 1975. "Owner Occupied Housing in the Revised CPI: A Review." August.

———. 1977. "The Measurement of Shelter Costs for Homeowners in the Revised Consumer Price Index: Summary." March.

11

Discussions of Ann Dougherty and Robert Van Order,
"Inflation and Housing Costs"; Larry Ozanne, "Expanding
and Improving the CPI Rent Component"; and
Robert Gillingham, John S. Greenlees, and
William S. Reece, "Measuring the Cost of Shelter
for Homeowners"

Lawrence DeMilner, first discussant

I was asked to comment on these papers from the perspective of my
own work which is concerned with the impact of policy changes on inflation. The conceptual problem of homeownership in the CPI and the effect
the current treatment has on the aggregate measure of consumer inflation
have been recognized for quite some time. What was once a somewhat
academic concern, however, has recently become a very political one, due
to the budget's response to the large changes in the CPI and the evidence
that the current CPI is a distorted measure of the cost of living.

At the Congressional Budget Office (CBO) we have done some totaling
up of the kinds of federal programs which are indexed to the CPI, and
count some 35 million Social Security recipients, some 3 million federal
military retirees, and additional minor programs that add more to that
number. There are, in addition, some 9 million wage earners in the
private sector whose wages are formally indexed to the CPI and there are

[The author is an analyst at the Congressional Budget Office.]

quite a few more who have various forms of informal indexation. Two years ago, BLS estimated that a 1 percent change in the CPI would trigger an increase of some 1 billion dollars in additional income flows. We have made more recent calculations that are confined to government programs alone and find that a 1 percent change in the CPI will now trigger nearly $2.0 billion in federal outlays at projected FY 1981 expenditure levels. So, the accuracy of the CPI is an issue of considerable importance.

The existence of distortion in the CPI introduced by this homeownership concept leads one to inquire about the size of the distortion. We have the advantage now of regular reporting on alternative homeownership concepts embodied in experimental CPI measures produced by BLS. The two that have received the most attention are first, the rental equivalence measure which is the concept and the actual data that are used for measuring personal consumption expenditure prices in the GNP accounts, and, second, the user cost concept. If you compare the published experimental indices using these two alternatives with the actual CPI you find that over the last five years, the rental equivalence measure would have led to an average CPI increase some 0.8 percent per year lower than we had with the official CPI. If you use the user cost alternative you get about a 0.7 percent average decrease in the CPI. If you look at the cumulative effect over just the last three years, the rental equivalence would have saved us about 4 percentage points on the price level, the user cost somewhat less, about 2.3 percentage points.

So the problem of what to do about the CPI is a very critical one. There appear to be some differences of opinion at this conference as to what would be the best solution, whether some form of rental equivalence or some form of a user cost ought to be adopted. Now it is in this budget policy framework that I look briefly through these papers.

The Van Order and Dougherty paper was very interesting. I found myself in general agreement with the conclusions, but I question (from the point of view of a policy analyst) the applicability of this work—whether it could be somehow utilized in computations of the CPI. I think the sensitivity of the measures developed there to price expectations speaks for itself. There are many ways that have been proposed for developing an empirical approach to the measure of price expectations. The approaches differ quite a bit and it is not at all clear how one chooses the best approach. As a consequence it is not very clear to me that this kind of approach would ever be very useful in modifying the CPI.

I was very glad to see the Ozanne paper. That kind of work must be done to pave the way for eventually resolving this issue. And the same remark goes for the paper by Gillingham, Greenlees, and Reece. I am very encouraged to see this program being undertaken by the BLS. It reflects the staff's concern over this problem. I would add that I found the argument on behalf of rental equivalence in a recent paper by Gillingham a rather persuasive one.

I would like to conclude by saying conferences like this one are very useful and very timely. Discussions like this should lead economists to a much better consensus on an operational solution to the problem of measuring homeownership costs in the CPI. As far as the timing of the solution, my own feeling is that the sooner you find a solution the better. But in particular if you do not implement the solution by June or July, it's going to cost the federal government an extra $3 billion. And if you don't change by this July, I would say take your time because if we actually encounter this long awaited recession there will probably be some cyclical impact on interest rates. Given the very large weight housing components have in the CPI, they are very likely to push down the current CPI relative to the rental equivalence based measure and perhaps the user cost measure as well. (You do not want to change horses at the peak of the distortion if it has a cyclical character.) It would be better to ride the same index on the downward portion of the cycle and make a change at the bottom. This means that you may have another year before it becomes optimal to make a change between these two measures.

Frank de Leeuw, second discussant

All of the approaches to measuring homeownership costs in the CPI have their pitfalls. The main point I want to make in this comment is that looking at the pitfalls of only one method may lead to unfortunate decisions about the best approach. Sometimes the current debate reminds me of the judge who is called on to decide between two contestants. After observing only the first one he says, "Stop, that's enough! The second one wins." In the current debate, some of those who look carefully at the official index for homeownership costs say, "Stop! The user cost approach wins." Some of those who have started looking carefully at how to implement the user cost approach are inclined to say, "This won't work; a rental equivalence approach wins." What I propose to do is to briefly list

[The author is chief statistician at the U.S. Department of Commerce.]

what I think the main pitfalls are in each of these three approaches and only then state my conclusions about the best way to proceed.

I have least to say about the current treatment of homeownership in the CPI. Hendershott and Van Order have both explained clearly and convincingly the problems of using before-income-tax rather than after-income-tax mortgage and property tax costs and neglecting expected capital gains. While some of the other criticisms of the CPI are exaggerated, I think these two are valid and serious.

One of the alternatives to current treatment, the user cost approach, has a different set of problems, as valuable recent BLS staff work has made clear. One problem is that the immediate effect of a reduction in income tax rates—apart from its later effect on economic behavior—is to reduce the tax advantages of homeownership and hence to raise after-tax user cost. The BLS staff would find it a real challenge to explain to the Joint Economic Committee that the cost of living increased last month because Congress had just cut tax rates. This paradox arises because the cost of living is measured before direct taxes such as income taxes; user-cost advocates would be making an exception in the case of owner-occupied housing, on the grounds that for this category taxes are directly linked to expenditures, as they are for sales and excise taxes (which are included in the CPI).

One way to remove the paradox would be to measure the cost of living generally after direct taxes, i.e., to count income taxes as part of the cost of living. Then a cut in income tax rates would reduce the cost of living, with the increased user cost of housing serving merely to offset a part of the reduction. The British government has recently begun to calculate a "tax-and-price" index which measures the cost of living after direct taxes. British experience, I believe, has demonstrated that a tax-and-price index is not without its own major conceptual problems.

A much simpler way of dealing with the paradox is to let the base-period weights for mortgage interest rates and property taxes represent after-tax benefits, but let the price indexes multiplied by those weights represent before-tax user costs. The general reduction in owner-occupant housing costs due to their favored tax treatment would then be reflected in a lower importance of housing in the overall cost of living index; but short-term changes in tax rates would not affect the index. That solution is not elegant, but I think it would work very well.

A second problem of the user cost approach is measuring expected capital gains. I think that we can improve some, but probably not very much, on the expedient of using a long moving average of past housing price changes as the BLS does in some of its new experimental measures. The Van Order procedures, it seems to me, have much less appeal. They are so volatile that they make even the total CPI rate of change look like a random walk at times.

A third problem of the user cost approach arises from the assumption (underlying the derivation of the user cost formula) that households are in equilibrium with respect to their consumption of housing services. If households are not in equilibrium (and surely even households in the aggregate can be out of equilibrium following an unexpected change in housing market conditions), then the return on housing equity can be above or below its normal relation to other rates of return. It seems to me that this uncertainty about the rate of return on equity is what leads Greenless and his colleagues to turn to a rental equivalence measure. This is not the way they explain the problem, but I think that it is equivalent to their statement, and that they have indeed identified a pitfall on the user cost approach.

The other alternatives to the current treatment of homeownership costs, the rental equivalence approach, uses observations of market rents for a sample of dwelling units whose characteristics (other than tenure) match those of the universe of owner-occupied units. Rental equivalence has not had nearly as much scrutiny as the other two approaches. Larry Ozanne's paper for this conference is therefore most welcome; but it does not persuade me that this approach is without its own problems.

The drawback that Ozanne emphasizes is the tendency of conventional rent indexes to miss gradual depreciation over time in housing services or neighborhood conditions, which really are changes in quantity but show up as changes in price. The Annual Housing Survey data that Larry uses may help overcome this problem, as well as other problems related to the introduction of new rental units into a rental price index. More work with Annual Housing Survey data should be encouraged. I note that a plot, by city, of Ozanne's results versus CPI homeownership cost changes reveals very little correlation.

There are other problems with the rental equivalence approach as well. One is that the tax treatment of landlords does differ from the tax treatment of owner-occupants; therefore, the rent a dwelling commands in the rental market should in general differ from its monthly value to an owner-occupant. Another problem is that there is some probability—it is very hard to guess its magnitude—of widespread rent controls sometime in the next few years. If rents are controlled, then being wedded to a rental equivalence approach to measuring homeownership costs would be most unfortunate. For these reasons, it is advisable to base a measure on the costs an actual homeowner incurs every month—his outlays for interest, amortization, property taxes, and so on.

All three approaches to measuring homeownership costs, in short, have serious problems. My own preference, after reviewing the pitfalls in all three, is for some variant of user cost, although I think continuing work on rental equivalence would also be valuable. User cost is conceptually clearer than the current treatment, and it has the advantage of being built up from actual expense items facing homeowners rather than assumed equivalent items facing renters. The recently published BLS alternative measure labeled "X2" is one attempt at measuring user cost, and has a lot to recommend it. But I think that two changes in the X2 measure would greatly improve it and would have a major impact on the results. The first is using weights based on after-income-tax rather than before-tax mortgage and property tax outlays—a change which would reduce the weight of homeownership in the overall CPI. The second is using price items interest rates rather than interest rates alone as the basis for the price index to be multiplied by the weight for mortgage costs. The user cost formula clearly implies multiplication of these elements, and it would be an easy change to make. With those two changes, I think an index resembling the "X2" alternative would be an important advance over the current homeownership component of the CPI.

12

PANEL DISCUSSION ON LONG-RUN
TRENDS AND POLICY IMPLICATIONS

Introduced by Kevin E. Villani

Several years ago we had a conference somewhat similar to this in which we invited academics to assess issues in housing finance. Ed Kane was a participant at that conference. There were two conclusions to that conference; and one was that it was inevitable that monetary policy would be invoked as a spearhead in the battle against inflation and eventually choke off mortgage credit in the housing industry. I don't need to say anything more about that.

The second conclusion of that conference was that we needed to do more work in the area of house prices and inflation, so that we could discuss how the tax system works with the inflation rate to affect the price and the affordability of housing. We did that. We reordered some of our research priorities and a number of other individuals and interested institutions also reordered their priorities, so that yesterday we were able to call in a panel of approximately 35 academic economists and government technicians to discuss these issues.

Part of my task for today was supposed to be to summarize some of the conclusions that these economists reached. In order to stay out of trouble

[The author is acting deputy assistant secretary for economic affairs, U.S. Department of Housing and Urban Development.]

137

with the people who presented papers, with the many discussants, and with the many, many critics, what I intended to say was that the conclusions were so stimulating and provocative and perhaps of such serious consequence that the tapes of that session have been impounded in the interest of national security. But of course that is not true. What really happened was that we confirmed the old maxim that if you laid all the economists in the world end to end in a line, they would not reach a conclusion; so I have very little to say in the way of a general summary.

But I will go back and summarize three points from three of the major papers. One of those, from the paper by Dougherty and Van Order, was that when you take into account the tax system and the capital gains from homeownership and recalculate the aggregate consumer price index, 25 percent of the rise in the CPI since 1967 is spurious. That is provocative! In another paper, Hendershott and Hu calculate the real after-tax rates of return on homeowner equity for various six-year intervals and conclude that homeowners realized a real after-tax rate of return that was anywhere from 3½ to 10½ percent greater than what they had expected when they bought those houses. Now that is a substantial multiple of the real rate of return that might have been expected when they bought. Moreover, these returns contrast sharply with the negative return that was earned on financial assets over that period. The paper by Hamilton and Cooke of Johns Hopkins University concludes that the price of housing services in real terms had declined at an annual rate of 3 percent a year for 25 years— from the beginning of 1950 to 1975.

To say the very least, these conclusions are all very provocative. I think one general conclusion of the panel and the general theme of the papers is that homeownership costs, as they calculate them, have been low because of the way inflation and taxes affect these costs, and I know I will have a lot of disagreement and dissenion about that.

What are some of the issues before the panel today in the area of house prices? One of them is the issue of affordability. That is, what do rising house prices imply both for first-time homebuyers and for people who are already in the market and who earn capital gains? What does it imply for the real cost of housing services?

Other sorts of issues that we talked about yesterday and that may receive some more attention today are measurement issues. How do we calculate what it really costs, how does that translate into a consumer price index, and what are the implications of the way we treat homeownership for the consumer price index, and the broader issue of indexing to the CPI?

A familiar theme in yesterday's discussion was the extent to which the capital gains on homeowner equity have reduced the national savings rate. That is, households perceived their rising capital gains and the rising net worth in the form of homeowner equity and increased their spending commensurate with their wealth. This may have been a major prop keeping the economy out of recession in the last several years. One of the major implications here is that if the perception of what is going to happen to home prices in the immediate future changes, then it may have very severe consequences for the performance of the economy in the short run. In the longer run, it may improve the prospects for increased capital formation. When we save in the form of homeownership and substitute that form for plant and equipment, productivity is reduced.

Another major issue is the potential for house prices to actually decline. The economists examined present value theories of house prices and determined that current price levels were supportable. Nevertheless, having seen declines in the price of silver and other speculative commodities, the hypothesis that perhaps house prices have been bid up beyond what more permanent factors would support needs careful consideration. A change in the perceptions of future inflation could dramatically alter the structure of house prices and there could be actual declines. There are a number of serious consequences; a decline in spending and an increase in mortgage default, to name a few.

Leo Grebler, panelist

I am going to use my allotted 15 minutes to discuss a policy issue that pertains to the past few years rather than the next few years. I am sure many people in the audience would rather have me engage in futurity than in a backward look, but I still have the illusion that experience is something important and worthwhile to study.

Here is the policy issue: did policy makers miss an opportunity by failing to use selective housing credit policies to restrain the 1976–1978 house price inflation?

There is no question that the financial system in those years accommodated the home-buying spree that inflated house prices. I do not have to

[The author is emeritus professor of Real Estate and Urban Land Economics, University of California.]

remind you that financial institutions, particularly savings and loans, were flush with deposits and were under great pressure to invest the incremental funds. The deposit inflow was fueled by public regulation in mid-1978 with the introduction of the so-called T-bill accounts. Another expansionary force in home financing was the extraordinary growth of mortgage-backed securities guaranteed by federal agencies. Mortgage pools grew from $8 billion in 1975 to $20 billion by 1977.

The net additions to the home mortgage debt rose from $41 billion in 1975 to $105 billion in 1978; a 155 percent increase in just three years. The share of residential mortgages in total borrowings by nonfinancial sectors also increased sharply during that period.

The point of reciting some of the data that are familiar to most of you is that in contrast to the usual complaint of underallocation of credit to the housing sector, it suggests the possibility of overallocating credit. This is the point made much more forcefully yesterday by Hendershott.

One of the factors in the spectacular growth was the vigorous expansion of homebuilding. Other factors were the surging purchases of existing homes and the escalation of house price which exceeded the rate of general inflation by very substantial margins. There has been widespread agreement that homebuying reflected not only normal market forces but the emergence of the single-family house as an asset effective in protecting people against inflation. Thus, inflationary expectations bolstered the credit demand for housing, which by tradition is a highly leveraged investment.

There is no evidence that lenders responded to booming housing demand by stiffening the noninterest terms of home loans. It was not until late 1978 and 1979 that average loan-to-value ratios of conventional mortgages were reduced and then not by an awful lot. Average maturities lengthened throughout the 1975-1979 period for mortgages on both new and existing property. There is also evidence that lenders allowed some stretching of the conventional relationships of house price to income and mortgage payments to income.

The first question is, could general monetary policy in this period, 1976-1978, successfully cope with the house price inflation? I don't think so. A general monetary policy sufficiently restrictive to moderate the house price inflation would have had disastrous macroeconomic effects. As it was, high nominal interest did not seem to deter home buying at all during the 1976-1978 period.

The second issue is whether specific housing credit restraints were called for. The rest of what I have to say revolves around this issue.

Policy makers had a wide variety of options. I present them in no particular order of preference. First, the authorities who supervised financial institutions could have issued cautionary statements backed by the warning that examiners would make a special effort to scrutinize lending practices very closely. Second, supervising authorities could have urged home mortgage lenders to join in voluntary credit control in order to avoid imposed controls. Third, the growth of mortgage-backed securities could have been slowed by rationing the volume of federal agency guarantees. Fourth, Federal National Mortgage Association (FNMA) and Government National Mortgage Association (GNMA) could have sold larger amounts of loans to sop up funds for residential mortgage investment. Fifth, Federal Home Loan Bank advances could have been restrained by raising interest rates and eligibility standards. The only measure of this type was taken in April 1977 by the Federal Home Loan Bank of San Francisco. Finally, selective credit controls could have been used for reducing maximum loan-to-value ratios and maximum maturities on home loans. To my nonlegal mind, the Credit Control Act of 1969 provided sufficient authority for that kind of action.

I do not know whether these options were considered, and if so, rejected. One might be inclined to attribute the failure to act to a recognition lag. The house price inflation appeared first in California and perhaps was shrugged off as a local or regional phenomenon. This explanation does not suffice for very long; the inflation soon spread rapidly to other areas and reached nationwide proportions. The hypothesis of a recognition lag is difficult to accept when one remembers that the boom in the house market was so well publicized.

Alternatively, policy makers may have shied away from selective credit restraint because of its difficulties. These are very real. In order to be fair and evenhanded, I will briefly mention at least some of the difficulties attached to each of the possible methods of constraint.

Cautionary pronouncement issued by the authorities might have gone unheeded. Or, if made public, they may even have had perverse effects on potential homebuyers. The prospect for voluntary credit control, it seems to me, was extremely poor. Rationing of government agency guarantees of mortgage-backed securities could have rechanneled some of the funds to other mortgage investors. Larger sales of loans from FNMA and GNMA would have entailed capital losses. In the case of GNMA, the losses would have been charged to the federal budget; but for FNMA losses would have impaired its earnings and capital base. It is difficult to reconcile those losses with the responsibilities to private stockholders.

Restraint on FHLB advances could have caused savings and loan associations to turn to commercial bank credit. In any event, this kind of restraint could have been pushed to the point where the savings and loan associations would have been unable to meet their outstanding loan commitments which were huge at that time.

Controls on noninterest terms on home loans were tried in two earlier periods—during the Korean War and in 1955–1956. These experiences were not encouraging. We learned that the political and administrative problems were formidable. They would have been compounded by the incidence of restrictive terms on homebuyers of moderate income whose access to the market was already diminishing. Thus, there would have been demand for exemptions for house price or borrowers' income criteria which might have been irresistible.

Nevertheless, it should be noted that the relatively low effectiveness of controls during the two episodes in the 1950s was at least partly due to special circumstances that were not replicated in 1976–1978. I refer to Jack Guttentag's analysis of the earlier experience. [1]

With all proper regard to the difficulties of selective credit restraint, I cannot help being impressed with the failure to use the substantial federal powers in residential financing for countercyclical action when boom conditions in the housing market clearly called for it. As on other occasions, policy makers opted for keeping the housing sector going at almost any cost.

We know now, and I think we might have predicted earlier, that the massive injection of credit into the housing market did not keep housing industry stable at all. We know for sure that it almost guaranteed the contrary—a high degree of instability.

The opportunity for housing credit restraint clearly vanished in 1979 when the surge of home buying subsided and the rate of house price advances began to decline. There was no point then in locking the barn after the horse had been stolen. At the same time, I feel that the episode of 1976–1978 remains instructive for future policy should inflationary expectations revive again and lead to another binge of home purchases and yet another round of house price inflation.

This brings us to the real subject of this morning's meeting. What about the future?

It seems to me that a good starting point for contemplating the future is to keep in mind that past housing boom. It was not an ordinary boom. It had the extra ingredient of a house price inflation not comparable to any house price inflations we have had in preceding peacetime housing booms.

One may expect that the slump in which we already find ourselves will not be just an ordinary slump—namely, a decline in new production. There is the threat of some house price deflation following upon the house price inflation.

Although I am a born optimist, I believe that this is indeed likely in the short run. We will have a slump with something extra added to it—some decline in house prices on average. This is to be expected because we have at least temporarily run out of people who will venture into the market in anticipation of negative real mortgage interest rates, say 10 percent nominal rates versus an expected annual appreciation of their house equity by 20 or 30 percent. The problem is compounded by the fact that even most of the recent homebuyers are sitting prettily on 7, 8, 9, or 10 percent mortgages and will find it very difficult to trade up at the much higher current interest rate.

In the short run, I think we are faced with some real problems. Now, how short is short? I cannot put a time dimension on this kind of thing. One reason is that a great deal may depend on the success or failure of what is currently being done in terms of monetary and fiscal policy. If the scenario postulates reasonable success of the present policy to reduce the rate of inflation and keep it reduced (which is the most important point), then we still have favorable demographic factors for homebuilding and an increase in the strategic age bracket for home purchase. We also have the prospect of homebuilding or residential construction in toto fostered by real income gains.

If, however, our present and any future policies should not succeed— and I feel constrained to include that in my array of scenarios—then we face a possibility of renewed inflation expectations and maybe a repitition of the experience of the past. We would then have a new cohort of homebuyers emulating the homebuyers of 1975–1978.

John C. Weicher, panelist

I am going to talk this morning about recent trends in housing affordability and homeownership, and their relationship to inflation, the most important phenomenon affecting homeownership. Like Leo Grebler, I am going to start with the past. I am a believer in Thornton Wilder's no-

[The author is director, Housing and Financial Markets Program, The Urban Institute.]

tion that we know less about the past than we know about the future. It is always useful to study what has happened to get some idea of what might happen next.

In the case of housing affordability and inflation, it is especially interesting to study the past, because the past is very much like the present. We have a popular notion that it is much harder to buy a house now than it used to be. That notion is itself not a new idea. People compare today's markets to the mid-1960s or the late 1960s. But if you will go back to that period and read what people were writing at that time, you find they were saying the same thing: it is harder to buy a house "today"—in 1965 or 1969—than it was "10 years ago"—in 1955 or 1959.

Indeed, you can trace this concern back to the late 1940s, right after the war. People were saying in 1949 it is very hard to buy a house and in 1939 it was much easier. That is interesting when you remember what the overall economy was like in 1939.

Reviewing the history of this notion, it appears that it has been getting harder to buy a home for over 30 years. This must be unique among consumer goods. The perception is strong, but it is also wrong by every measure of housing quantity that we have. We know we are living in bigger houses with more amenities than right after the war or even 10 years ago.

There is another interesting and relevant point about the history of this idea. The perception that it is much harder to buy a house now than it used to be is much stronger when we are in a period of unusual inflation by historical standards. Compared to today's inflation, the mid-1960s and late 1960s now look like golden years. We have forgotten that then there was rather rapid inflation by the standards of time. You may remember that in 1968 Richard Nixon was campaigning against 3 or 4 percent inflation, which was thought to be much worse than the rate of about 1 or 1½ percent that we endured in the mid-1960s.

If you go back to the late 1940s there was very rapid inflation in the postwar period, exacerbated by the fact that we had price controls during the war which postponed inflationary pressures.

What we seem to observe is a kind of money illusion. You see your income go up in an inflationary period. You think that you can buy a house with this year's income where you couldn't last year. It is true that with this year's income you can buy a house at last year's price. But you cannot buy it at this year's price, if both price and income have gone up merely as a result of inflation and you could not buy it previously.

That brings me to the effects of inflation on the housing market. There are a number of major effects; I will focus on six of them.

First, the most noticeable, is what inflation does to the home you want to buy. The Census Bureau and the newspapers report the price of new homes every month; I think this is the main source of public concern over affordability. (There is much less attention paid to existing home prices.) The new home price is either a record high or close to a high every month.

Over the 11 years from 1967 to 1978, the price of the typical new home increased by 135 percent. That is a substantial rate of 10 percent compounded annually for an 11-year period, but it is not unique among items in the Consumer Price Index. The price of oil has certainly gone up that fast or faster; utilities have gone up that fast; and there are individual commodities which have gone up at a rather rapid rate.

But inflation does something else in the housing market which is unique; it drives up the mortgage interest rate. In 1967 the mortgage interest rate was about 9 percent and inflation was about 6. Today they are running about 16 and 13, respectively.

The combined effect of the mortgage interest rate and the home purchase price is to drive up the monthly payment rather drastically. For example, assuming a constant down payment, the current monthly payment on the typical new home at the new high interest rate would have gone up by 230 percent as compared to 1967.

These are the negative effects of inflation. If you concentrate on them, you probably conclude that nobody can afford to buy a house today. Who can afford to pay three and one-half times what they were paying 11 years ago? But there have been some positive effects as well.

First, inflation drives up income by almost as much as it drives up home prices. In that same 11-year period, the median family income has gone up by 122 percent, less than the 135 percent of the typical new home price, but not so very much less.

Second, if you own a house, inflation drives up the price of the home you want to sell as well as the price of the home you want to buy. The typical existing home sold went up in price by 150 percent in the 11-year period, faster than the price of the typical new home.

This is important because all of the increase in the existing home accrues to the homeowner as an increase in equity. Thus, the effect of inflation on your wealth is rather dramatic. If you bought the typical new home in 1967 and sold it in 1978, your equity in the home went up just short of sixfold in those 11 years. Very crude calculations indicate that the rate of return on your down payment works out to something over 18 percent a year, compounded over an 11-year period.

These calculations mean that, if you were a new-home buyer in 1967, you could sell that now-old home in 1978, put the equity down on another new home, and meet the conventional—formerly immutable—rule of thumb of spending no more than 25 percent of your income on housing. Even with the higher mortgage rate, even with the higher cost of utilities, even with higher property taxes, even with every other cost increase, you could still buy a much better new home than the one you sold. The figures indicate that the home you buy would have a couple of hundred square feet more than the home you sell; it would probably have a two-car garage instead of a one-car garage; it would probably have a fireplace where the home you sold probably didn't.

It is true that only the current homeowner benefits from the increase of equity on an existing home. The current renter is on the wrong side of that increase. But homeowners comprise just less than two-thirds of all households; and they have been at least 60 percent of all households during this entire period of inflation.

This kind of calculation indicates why people want to buy, not just why they can buy. Once you own a home, you are hedged against inflation for a substantial part of your wealth. Despite the increase in the other costs, you can reasonably expect to move, if you want to, in a few years.

Now, there is a flaw in this picture: while almost two-thirds of us own our own home, about one-third of us don't. If you have been renting during this period of inflation and you want to buy a home, you are in trouble. For you, it has been much harder to buy the home that you want.

There are some groups in our society which are predominantly renters: the poor, racial minorities, city dwellers, the unmarried, nontraditional households, and young families. Most of them apparently are having increasing difficulty in becoming owners.

For example, if you look at the incidence of homeownership across the income distribution, holding real income constant, you find that the rate of ownership is up from 1970 to 1977 for every income group—except one. That one is the poorest group, people with incomes of less than $5,000 in 1970 and $8,000 in 1977, amounting to a little more than a quarter of all households. For them and only for them, ownership is down a little bit, from about 50 percent to about 48 percent.

If you look at racial minorities, you get an interesting pattern. Homeownership was increasing for blacks and for Hispanics—up to 1976 or 1977, then it decreased. Whether this very recent decline is just a squiggle or the start of a trend, we do not yet know.

For city dwellers, homeownership has been decreasing since 1975; for city dwellers who are minorities, it has been decreasing, faster, since about 1975.

For the unmarried, the nontraditional household, the ownership rates have been dropping, in some cases rather substantially, during the 1970s. Declining rates apply to both male-headed households and female-headed households.

The exception to this pattern is young families. For married couples with the head of household under age 30, the incidence of ownership went up from about 40 percent of those households in 1970 to just short of 50 percent in 1977. This is the fastest growth rate for any demographic group. It started from a lower base than most others; but adjusting for that, it is still the fastest rate of growth for any group.

Now that is interesting. Who do you hear about in Washington as having trouble buying a home? It is not the really poor. It isn't often the minorities. It is that young family that cannot possibly get the money for the down payment because the family does not have any assets. I heard proposals to help the young family in particular all during the latter part of the 1970s—all during the period when the numbers tell us that their homeownership rates have been increasing.

The housing market behavior for the young family is quite interesting. If you look at what the Annual Housing Survey and other authoritative sources tell us about people who are buying homes, you find that in the mid-1970s close to 10 percent of the young families every year were buying a house. In 1977 the rate went over 15 percent. We do not yet know what happened in 1978.

An important question is how the young people are finding the down payment. There isn't much hard data; we have a lot of anecdotes and a lot of hypotheses. Are they able to save up quickly because there are two people working? Are they getting the money from their parents? Some of the older people in this audience have suggested that as an explanation to me. Are they stealing it? We just do not have the information.

But we do know what they do when they get the down payment, wherever they get it from. They generally buy one of the less expensive older homes on the market or one of the least expensive new homes. They get on the homeownership-inflation ladder; they put themselves in a position to benefit from inflation through the appreciation of their homes; and ultimately they trade up to the bigger and newer homes just like their elders have been doing during this inflation.

At the end of last year, a reporter asked me what the decade of the 1980s will look like in housing. I thought then, and I think now, that it was a remarkably bad time to make a prediction. We do not know for sure whether the Federal Reserve is serious this time about bringing inflation under control. But if the Federal Reserve is serious, I think you will see some decline in prices. I do not know how large it might be. It is conceivable that it might be just a pause in the rate of growth, but it is more likely to be a decline because of the importance of inflationary psychology supporting current price levels.

If it turns out that the Fed is not serious, that it eases up, or it is perceived to ease up, then I think we are going to have another boom in house prices. It will be something like the third or fourth time in the decade that we will have made a pass at bringing the rate of inflation under control and quit before accomplishing anything. We will draw the appropriate lesson from that experience: there will be a much more rapid price increase than Leo Grebler suggested.

Edward J. Kane, panelist

Philosophers emphasize that the conceptual categories in which we think affect what we actually see. It is hard to grasp an event for which our mind has not already established a conceptual place in which to store the image being observed. The accompanying cartoon is intended to dramatize this point and to begin to apply it to our subject. It is a picture of an animal doing something. Without looking ahead, try to guess exactly what is doing what? (No prizes will be awarded.)

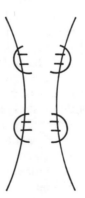

[The author is Reese professor of banking and monetary economics, The Ohio State University.]

Although my draftsmanship is a bit crude, I sought to picture a bear climbing the far side of a tree. Given the effects of the ongoing credit crunch in U.S. housing activity, a few more trees exist in the nation's forests this spring than hibernating bears must have expected to encounter as they woke up in their caves.

What Have We Learned during the 1970s about Housing and Inflation?

Although they do not precisely have front and back sides, assets can be viewed from two perspectives, too. This is because they serve their owners both as consumption goods and as investment goods. They produce simultaneous flows of consumption and investment services to their owners. Over the last decade, economic analysis of housing demand has shifted from the familiar conceptual categories of consumption theory to the subtler perspectives of investment theory. Today's economic literature portrays purchasers of housing—not as allocating a periodic income over a set of current consumption opportunities—but as allocating their human and nonhuman wealth across opportunities for investment and current consumption. This shift in point of view has enormous implications for public policy. It focuses attention on how accelerating inflation impacts on a long-neglected policy gap: the differential between the *an*ticipated *r*eal *a*fter-*t*ax rate of return (or "A-RATE") on leveraged investment in housing and the A-RATE available on alternative receptacles for household saving. The term "A-RATE" offers a dual mnemonic. First, it stands for "adjusted rate," where the abbreviation is also an acronym built up from the first letters of the conceptual adjustments an investor must make to render nominal interest rates intelligible. For poetic effect I chose to augment these letters with a silent E. Second, it designates the academic grade I feel this interest-rate concept deserves relative to previous explanations of the 1970s' housing boom.

After allowing for possible differences in risk, a family's saving tends to flow to the set of assets that offers the best A-RATE to households in its economic and demographic circumstances. To appreciate why A-RATEs should govern the allocation of household savings, we need only to grasp two straightforward ideas. First, we must recognize that, since investors cannot forecast future prices perfectly, they must allocate wealth on the basis of *anticipated* returns. Second, we must recognize the usefulness of adjusting dollar returns on different assets for simultaneous "bites" put on these returns by inflation and by taxes. Rates of return taken net of the bite taken by inflation are called "real" returns. Subtracting the further bite taken by taxes gives real after-tax returns.

In the 1970s and except for America's wealthiest households, five conditions made the A-RATE on leveraged investments in housing seem better than A-RATEs on financial investments:

1. The services a house provides its owners are not taxed at all.

2. Until the last few months, increases in house prices regularly outran the overall rate of inflation.

3. The discounted present value of capital-gains taxes on price appreciation in owner-occupied housing is negligible.

4. Mortgage interest rates were kept low by public policy.

5. Nominal rates of return on low-denomination financial assets were pressed down by deposit-rate ceilings.

As a result, A-RATEs on housing frequently exceeded 5 percent, while those on the financial instruments traditionally used by America's small savers were negative for at least the past decade. Because of the A-RATE gap, many families who for personal reasons might have preferred to rent their homes have discovered that financially they could not "afford" to pass up the investment opportunity provided by homeownership.

Once one understands the A-RATE concept—just as when one finally sees the more subtle image in a perspective-reversal drawing such as our "bear climbing a tree"—things never look the same again. The relationship between housing and inflation is suddenly recognized to be circular. Increases in housing demand remain a cause of inflation. But at the same time accelerations in inflation can be seen to make housing demand more buoyant.

Over the last 15 years, small savers increased their demand for housing precisely because this was the most promising way to preserve their savings against the twin scourges of inflation and income taxes. To understand the age and wealth distributions of differential rates of return, we must focus on the interaction of inflation with taxation and regulation. The A-RATE gap varies across individual tax brackets. It also varies with a household's accumulated wealth. Because U.S. deposit markets are closely regulated, accelerating inflation makes the A-RATE gap enormous for young households and households with average or below-average wealth.

Where Do We Go from Here?

To project where the profession will go from here, we must identify important conceptual elements neglected in the A-RATE analysis. What finance-theory concepts and models deserve to be incorporated into the standard analysis of the inflation-and-housing story? Two areas of neglect stand out: (1) how to measure and analyze the portfolio risk associated with housing investment, and (2) how to model the supply side of the housing industry, with special emphasis on the effect of rising costs of energy on construction techniques, home design, and the distribution of land prices.

ELEMENTS OF PORTFOLIO RISK IN HOUSING

Deflation Risk One way government officials could reduce the A-RATE gap is to slow the overall rate of inflation. Trends observed in home prices during the 1970s lulled many households into the naive belief that, in an inflationary environment, a home is virtually a riskless investment. But homeownership does not protect against inflation per se, only against unanticipated inflation. What must be recognized is that during the 1970s housing offered such good protection against inflation only because U.S. monetary policy was expansionary enough to cause unexpectedly accelerating inflation.

Home prices had to rise faster than the rate of inflation throughout the 1970s, primarily because political pressure on the Federal Reserve kept the A-RATE very low on financial assets. Every time inflation accelerated unexpectedly, housing prices had to rise even faster to force the A-RATE that homes offered marginal investors down to the same low level.

Since October 6, 1979, the Federal Reserve has endeavored to maintain substantial positive A-RATEs on financial assets. To bring the A-RATE on housing up to this new level, the rate of housing-price increases has had to slow. In fact, when the cash flows accepted in seller-issued second mortgages is properly discounted, I believe that one can show that nominal home prices have in many parts of the country actually eased and, as the implications of this for risk assessment are increasingly recognized, housing prices may ease a little more. On the other hand, if unemployment rises sharply, I believe that political pressures will make it impossible in the short run for the Fed to maintain high A-RATEs on long-term financial assets. Although the reaction might be delayed, this would eventually push the rate of increase in housing prices above the overall rate of U.S. inflation again.

Situational Risk   This analysis indicates that housing investments bear considerable deflation risk. It is careless to describe housing as a "hedge" against inflation. For most of us, it is actually a "speculation" on accelerating inflation, one that during the 1970s the U.S. Bureau of Inflation turned into an excellent bet.

What housing truly hedges against is best described as "situational risk." Every family faces a lifetime need for an uncertain stream of housing services. From a financial point of view, this stream of future needs constitutes a liability that may be assigned a risk-adjusted present value. Other things equal, the amount and quality of housing space demanded probably increases with a household's expected family size and wealth just as aggregate housing needs vary with aggregate wealth and demographic factors. Although lower mortality rates and contemporary techniques of birth control tend to make the modern family's future housing needs less uncertain than in previous generations, irregular couplings and uncouplings (and therefore "household formations") have become distinctly less predictable.

Purchasing one's home establishes a more secure option on the future occupation of the given dwelling unit and (particularly, when financed by means of a fixed-rate mortgage) places a lid on the dollar amount of some very important elements of the future costs of being housed. It may be useful also as a plan of forced saving and as a way of balancing the inflation risk inherent in a household's pension plan and financial-asset portfolio. At the same time, homeownership subjects one to risks of changing family size, neighborhood quality, operating expenses, and commuting costs. "Modest" home purchases are on balance, hedging transactions. For society as a whole, the problem is that the A-RATE gap has encouraged household after household to purchase homes that are up-sized and overequipped.

Social-Priority Risk   Policy makers can attack either side of the A-RATE gap. Precisely because in the U.S. housing is taxed and regulated preferentially relative to other household assets, future prices of homes are exposed to the risk of unfavorable reorientations in regulatory policy or in the tax structure. In fact, the more housing booms, the weaker the case for continuing to tax and regulate it preferentially. Conversely, when housing runs into trouble, pressures for helping the construction industry grow.

This dialectical process of social priorities being undermined by their success and strengthened by their failures stands out sharply in the case of what is called "tax-bracket creep." As Pat Hendershott illustrates in developing policy implications from his analysis, accelerating inflation tends both to raise a household's marginal income-tax rate and to increase pressure for tax and regulatory reform. Higher marginal tax rates improve the short-run competitive position of a tax- preferred asset (such as owner-occupied housing) relative to more heavily taxed financial assets. But at the same time they generate political pressure against the long-run survival of the favored assets' differential tax preference. Inflation-induced inequities in the distribution of A-RATEs lead the public and elected officials to reevaluate the tax structure and to modify household saving and investment incentives. Looking toward the future, the tax exemption just granted to interest income and the new financial-reform act are tiny steps toward closing the favorable A-RATE gap that in the U.S. housing has long enjoyed relative to deposit assets. Although I doubt that in my lifetime the lawyers in Congress will dare to tackle the problem of taxing the in-kind services a house provides its owners, I see a substantial chance that Congress will eventually reduce the extent to which mortgage interest is deductible for high-income households.

ENERGY PRICES AND THE DISTRIBUTION OF LAND PRICES WITHIN METROPOLITAN AREAS

To explain the influence of factor prices on housing supply, it is natural for economists to assume an unchanging production function. At the margin of metropolitan development, land is balanced between agricultural and suburban uses. When food prices soar, it becomes harder to bid farm land away to suburban uses. Moreover, when energy prices rise faster than the rate of inflation, higher and less certain expected costs of suburban commuting reduce the demand for converting land away from farming.

What we observe then is a sharp change in the location gradient and an increased density of land use in the near suburbs. Central-city and close suburban properties become more valuable relative to residential property in the distant suburbs. In city after city, this is greatly changing the income pattern of residence, leading to the rapid gentrification of energy-efficient row houses in formerly blighted neighborhoods. To model this, housing analysts need to develop data and concepts that would break out the supply and demand for land separately from the supply and demand for structures. Energy-efficient structures and locations figure to have a brighter future than other types.

Lawrence Simons, panelist

Normally, I would feel a little out of place sitting around the table with academic economists, but not when the subject is housing and housing finance.

I find very little to disagree with in the assumption that the demand for housing is now being stimulated by forces other than the need for shelter. It is really being stimulated by the investment opportunities that housing affords. That subject has been discussed thoroughly this morning.

First, I have heard mentioned only twice this morning the demand side for housing in this country. I think it is important to point out that the most conservative predictions estimate that we will need 20–22 million units during the decade of the eighties to fulfill the demand for housing for the growing population of this country. The United States is not like many other countries which have fairly static populations. Their housing problems and their housing policies must reflect that type of situation. But we are still a growing country with a rapidly expanding age group which will be demanding housing in the eighties. We must deal with the problem of housing recognizing that there is this strong demand. Government policy must recognize that. When you do not satisfy the demand, you force house prices up. I think the past policies of this country have tried to recognize this fact in a countercyclical way.

The classic way in which we structured housing finance in this country made the resources for housing credit very susceptible to credit controls. It does not matter what we call it—credit controls or monetary policies—we knew what the effects on housing credit would be. We knew when we started raising short-term interest rates that banks could not handle it. We knew that the thrift institutions would lose money and housing finance would suffer.

It was not only a question of high interest rates, it was a lack of availability of money. The results were an industry whose record of performance looked like ski slopes—ski slopes down and ski lifts up. As a builder and as one who studies the situation, I can say that these policies led to a very inefficient industry. It led to an industry which could not gear up to the high side, and which took a tremendous beating on the low side. Every time the production of housing units goes above 2 million, the manufacturers are not equipped to supply the necessary goods. Based on

---

[The author is former assistant secretary for housing, and FHA commissioner, U.S. Department of Housing and Urban Development.]

my experience as a builder, I can tell you that when times were good, you could not get bathroom fixtures to finish houses, because industry just could not keep up with the demand. When times were bad, you could not turn the flow of materials off. Manufacturers became very conservative about making capital investments to increase the supply of materials. I remember talking to the manufacturers of insulation in 1977 and trying to encourage them to expand their supply side to meet the oncoming crisis. They were very reluctant to invest the necessary capital. They wanted to see a definite, firm ongoing government policy which would result in a permanent demand for insulation goods.

There is also the labor problem. Every time the building industry turned off sharply, unemployment climbed. People left the industry. And once they left it, they never wanted to come back. The result is that we have a very inefficient housing industry.

If you look at it in the broad policy sense, this administration tried to cushion the cycles that the industry faced. The administration tried to minimize the cyclicality by using the affordability factor rather than the availability factor. This approach resulted in the money market certificate and led to the expanded use of GNMA mortgage-backed securities as well as FNMA and all secondary markets.

The decision was made that the contraction for housing should emerge from the affordability factor. This would be a natural effect and would be reflective of the total economy. It did work. It worked very well. In 1979 with historically high interest rates, the industry produced 1,750,000 units. Retail sales of existing units also held up strongly.

Unfortunately, housing prices also held up. Why? That is a question which has been discussed at length. It reminds me of a visit to Buenos Aires, Argentina a year ago. It was a period of very high inflation. As I walked through the city one afternoon, I saw buildings under construction all over the city. No one was working on them. I asked my host if this was a holiday? He said, "No, this isn't a holiday." I responded, "Why aren't they working on these buildings?" He said, "These aren't buildings; these are individual savings accounts."

This is what was happening in Argentina. As soon as people had available cash, they would buy the land. The next time they had the available cash, the foundation would go in. And so on. This is the type of situation I fear most.

Classically, in an inflationary society real estate has always been looked upon as a great hedge against that inflation. It has been viewed as something to speculate on like commodities. I think that is bad. As a

builder I think it is bad and for the country I think it is bad. Before this inflationary period the demand side reflected shelter needs. People made
housing choices based on what they could afford and what their needs
were. Most had the opportunity to make choices. Government policy was
to provide people with these opportunities.

Housing was always regarded as a safe thing to buy, if you could afford
it. Not because it was going to be your substitute savings account, but
because the demand for housing would remain strong. One could expect
some appreciation in the value of housing. Back then the appreciation
value of a house was between 6 and 8 percent a year. I think that was the
usual way that people looked at housing. Today, when appreciation rates
are at 17 and 18 percent, housing is viewed as an investment. People are
now allocating far more of their resources for their shelter needs than ever
before.

I have listened to the scenario that has been played out by Leo Grebler
and John Weicher. I agree that there is a possibility in the future that we
may get into some trouble. The groundwork is there. But I do not believe
it will happen. I think what we are already seeing is a slowdown in housing
prices as the government's inflation policy takes hold. Unless there is a
total economic disaster in this country such as prolonged deep recession or
depression, housing prices will slow down. They may show a very nominal
increase again, but that would not be disastrous to the housing industry.
The question of affordability is really the whole issue.

Where do we go in the eighties and what do we look at? There are some
very serious issues which need to be examined and resolved. The first is
the source of housing credit. I think the whole thrift industry is in the
throes of a most difficult situation. We have finally realized that borrowing short to lend long cannot be profitable. The fragility of our economy
and the volatility of it leaves the thrifts in a very exposed position. We
must face the issue of whether or not we preserve the thrift industry as the
classic source of housing finance. We must decide to look at other sources
such as general market areas that are topped by mortgage-backed
securities and FNMA as a major source of housing finance.

If we do make that choice, what will be the impact on the thrift industry, the whole savings concept within our economy, and other major
credit markets? One alternative may be to preserve the thrift institutions
as the major means of housing credit. To do that, we will need to change
the form of the mortgage instrument radically. If we follow this course,
there is no question we would remove the A-RATE factor from housing.
Once you have indexed the mortgage rate to inflation, the whole A-RATE

factor comes out of it. But then if we take out that A-RATE factor, what happens to housing demand? What are the housing choices? Are we able to provide other housing choices for people as they stop seeking family homeownership? Going to a variable-rate mortgage has the threat of impairing the ability to become a homeowner.

I also have to examine the issue of whether alternative mortgage instruments feed inflationary expectations thereby causing the problem. The whole question of indexing housing finance is a very serious one, and that is really what I am talking about.

We also need to examine factors other than financing. I think that Ed Kane started to refer to the issues. What can we do to reduce the costs of housing, aside from the price of the structure. I believe you will see some very dramatic things taking place in the eighties. Unfortunately, land prices from a builder's point of view are really the residual cost of housing. They are determined by what the market will pay for the housing. You take the construction cost out and the cost of financing out, and you have a residual—the land. If you are the owner of undeveloped land that you have held in inventory for some time, you expect to make a profit on the land.

If you have to buy the land, you will pay exactly what the seller figures you can afford to pay for it and sell a house and make a profit. And I agree with Ed Kane that the controlling factor is changes in demography.

Given current energy problems, and the availablity of land in older urban areas, you will see the tremendous movement back into the inner cities. It is already happening, and it is encouraged by our national policy of the conservation of our resources. As this movement accelerates, that market demand will escalate prices.

There are things we can do in the area of building codes and in the matter of infrastructure required for the development of houses. The whole regulatory process is one that is going to come under very serious scrutiny. As a builder my experience with local government officials in the past three years has been very interesting. To me, the enemy of the industry was local government. Early in the administration I was asked to meet with the Housing Task Force of the U.S. Conference of Mayors. I went to the meeting kicking and screaming. The mayors talked to me about Community Development Block Grants and Section 312 loans. I talked to them about FHA insurance and 235 and investment in multifamily housing. Neither one of us understood each other.

Today, three years later, when I meet with these mayors, they are the ones who are talking to me about credit for multifamily and single-family housing. They are tuned-in to housing today. They realize that they have a responsibility and an opportunity to make development take place within their cities and their territorial jurisdictions in a rational way.

Local officials are prepared to play a major role. What they need is direction and support. The federal government is prepared to do this. I predict that in many areas the barriers for lower price housing will start coming down very rapidly. Some call it higher density; I call it the removal of the barriers.

I believe that one other area where you will see some major changes in housing is the energy area. This country has a major responsibility to respond to the energy crisis. The housing industry has a primary role to play in this area. I think residential construction today consumes about 22 percent of the nation's total energy consumption. The opportunities for conservation are very ample. I believe conservation will accelerate and will be stimulated by financial techniques and mechanisms.

Kevin, I appreciate the opportunity to participate in this conference. I would just like to reemphasize how much I agree with you that the question of inflation as it relates to housing prices is perhaps the most serious question the housing industry faces today.

Craig Swan, panelist

The focus of the discussions yesterday and today has been housing and inflation—both an understanding of the impacts of inflation on housing and some projections as to what is likely to happen in the future. Much of the discussion has appropriately concentrated on the clear benefits that have been occurring to homeowners from inflation.

I want to first mention some negative aspects of recent experience with inflation, especially variability in the rate of inflation which seems to be a fact of life.

One negative aspect relates to the uncertainty induced by fluctuations in the rate of inflation: is this only a temporarily higher rate of inflation, or have we reached a new plateau from which the rate of inflation may increase further? As expectations of inflation get built into interest rates, borrowers face similar concerns about interest rates. Are interest rates about to decline so I'll be better off if I wait, or in two years will I kick

[The author is associate professor of economics, University of Minnesota.]

myself for not borrowing at what will ex post be seen as very advantageous rates?

The difficulty of forecasting appears to be the major concern this morning. I imagine that for 1974 and other similar periods the record will show that the same concerns were raised: have we reached the point where the federal government is going to stick to its guns in terms of bringing down the rate of inflation, or is the rate of inflation simply going to ratchet up again?

A second major negative aspect of our experience with inflation relates to its impacts on thrift institutions. Many feel that fluctuations in actual rates of inflation have induced fluctuations in expected inflation and interest rates thus adding to the problems of thrift institutions. As market interest rates rise, thrifts feel pressure to pay competitive rates. With the introduction of the six-month money market certificates these pressures are even more direct. The result is severe disintermediation, a real risk of bankruptcy, and the possibility of financial chaos.

Inflation related problems of thrifts lead to the third negative aspect of recent experience, the continuing need for elaborate forms of first aid, in particular the series of ad hoc federal policies to fight first one crisis and then another. There is a risk that, in the aggregate and over time, these decisions will prove to be unwise. With attention focused on the immediate crisis, there is little time to consider the long-run, cumulative effects of these policy decisions. The six-month money market certificate is a case in point.

Turning now to the future, let me preface my remarks by saying that when I first go to Minnesota, Walter Heller told me, if you are going to make a forecast, give a number or a date, but never both. In regard to housing prices, I do not want to give either a number or a date. I would like to discuss the potential impacts of declines in income and the rate of inflation in a recession on housing markets, both in terms of quantities and prices.

With regard to income declines, I do not expect anything different to occur with respect to housing in this recession than has occurred in other postwar recessions. In particular, I do not foresee a repeat of the 1930s with widespread inability to make mortgage payments. Housing decisions are based on permanent income. Consumer expectations of their long-run income positions should show only small fluctuations if the future holds a traditional postwar recession. I see no reason to expect any other type. The net impact might be a small income-related decline in construction activity and a small income-related decline in the rate of increase of house prices. Let me be clear in saying that I do not foresee an income-related decline in nominal house prices, only the possibility of a slightly lower growth rate.

With regard to the rate of inflation, there is the potential for greater impacts. If I understand the thrust of Leo Grebler's, John Weicher's, and Ed Kane's remarks, they are forecasting declines in nominal house prices. It is certainly a headline-grabbing forecast, as I interpret their remarks as implying the potential for widespread declines in nominal house prices, not just isolated examples. Declines in nominal house prices could only come from a massive shift in either the demand or supply curve. I assume that no one is forecasting the appropriate shift in the supply curve. To lower nominal prices in the face of an unchanged demand curve, the supply curve would have to shift to the right, perhaps through a technological breakthrough that dramatically lowers costs. But note that such a shift also increases the level of production or at least increases production from what it otherwise would be if the demand curve is simultaneously shifting to the left. The concern this morning is with recession, not expansion.

Of more concern is a shift of the demand curve to the left. Major demand shifters would be income, population, other prices, and the rate of inflation. I have already briefly mentioned the impact of a recession-induced, temporary decline in real income. I see little reason to expect a major shift in the demand curve from this factor. Yesterday, Jim Kearl, and this morning Larry Simons, reminded us of the tremendous increase in the demand for housing from basic demographic factors. Household formation has continued at high rates. The baby boom babies are now leaving college and demanding their own housing units. I see little reason to expect any decline in the demand for housing from demographic factors.

The demand for housing does depend upon relative prices. Abstracting for the moment from the rate of inflation and the tax treatment of capital gains, increases in the level of nonhousing prices reduce the relative price of housing, shift the demand curve for housing, and lead to an increase in house prices. The increase in nonhousing prices is also likely to increase the cost of producing houses, thus shifting the supply curve. The result might well be an increase in house prices that matches the increase in other prices. This same argument works in reverse. That is, a decline in nonhousing prices would shift demand and supply curves down, leading to reduced housing prices. Thus a widespread deflation in prices would also lead to a deflation of housing prices. But let me emphasize that I am talking about actual declines in the price level, not a decline in a positive rate of increase from say 15 to 10 percent.

The one factor I have not yet discussed is the rate of inflation. The focus of much of the discussion yesterday was how special tax treatment of owner-occupied housing gives additional incentives to the demand for owner-occupied housing in inflationary periods. This additional incentive is above and beyond the impact of a change in the level of prices. As just discussed, a change in the level of prices would call for increases in house prices about equal to the increases in other prices. When one takes account of the special tax treatment of capital gains on houses, there is reason to expect a further shift in the demand curve. This is what Ed Kane talked about—the jacking up of house prices in order to get the A-RATE down low enough. If current house prices include a substantial inflation premium based on the expectation that inflation will continue at current high rates, then a decline in the rate of inflation, sufficient to change expectations, might lead to a fall in nominal house prices. Thus, important questions relate to the extent of inflationary expectations and the extent of any inflationary premium in current house prices.

I think there is a strong case to be made that if there is an inflation-induced premium in house prices, it is, for the most part, reflected in land prices. Unfortunately, the currently available data on house and land prices are not good enough to get a firm handle on this question. There is a pressing need for better data on house prices and in particular land prices.

If I were going to make a prediction, I might see some decline in the relative price of housing, especially if the federal government is consistent about reducing the long-run rate of inflation. But frankly, I find it hard to believe there will be a drop in nominal house prices. The possible elimination or moderation of any inflation premium would be taking place in an environment of continuing inflation. With inflation at 12 percent, it is pretty easy to make relative price adjustments without having any price fall. Remember that the government's official forecast for inflation is 12 percent for the year, not zero, and no one is seriously forecasting inflation will end next year. A gradual deceleration of inflation will allow ample time for an adjustment of relative prices without any decline in nominal house prices.

13

THE HIGH COST OF TRYING TO HELP HOUSING

Henry C. Wallich

While I have not had time really to look very closely at the fine papers contributed for this meeting, I did get the sense that people are beginning to think in terms of real interest rates after taxes. You have no idea what a hard concept that is to put across. Once somebody sees that, he is not going to be talking about high interest rates very much thereafter. What he might talk about are rates that are enormously uncertain and have a very different effect for different people.

I do not need to remind you that the real interest rate is after expected inflation, not after current inflation. There seems to be a peculiar tendency for the interest rate always to keep up pretty much with existing inflation, not just in the United States but in other countries as well. Now why isn't it inflation after taxes that the interest rate keeps up with? I do not know, but it does not seem to be the case. Maybe some research could be done here.

Another thing I do not need to remind you of is that "after taxes" poses the question "whose taxes?" For tax-exempt investors, most rates have remained marginally positive as inflation and interest rates have risen. Taxable investors, for the most part, have negative real rates after tax.

[The author is a member of the Board of Governors, Federal Reserve System.]

163

For somebody living in New York in the 70 percent top federal bracket, plus I think 14 percent New York State income tax, and I think 3½ percent city tax, and all experts can tell us which tax is deductible from which, a 20 percent interest rate loan for him or her is a flea bite. But take a poor constructor whose firm has had no profits for a year, he's hit with prime plus 3—that is a very different animal.

So what we have is essentially a distribution of impacts of the interest rate that is very uneven. Monetary policy may be hitting in some places so hard that it goes beyond endurance, before it begins to reach those that are relatively well protected by taxes. This is one of the difficulties I see to the concept of real interest rates after tax. But nevertheless, I think we have to hammer away at this concept; otherwise, we are not going to make people understand what the interest rates really mean today.

I was impressed by reading the long list of aid to housing. We have done, it seems to me, things for housing and for the housing finance industry that fall into two categories. One is of the structural kind working through taxes principally, but also through other institutional devices. The other is of a cyclical kind. The Federal Reserve has had something to do with the latter. On the structural side, we have had the tax deduction. Bear in mind that our way of treating homeowner interest is different, I think, from the practice in other countries. In other countries, interest payments are either not deductible at all or limited to some extent, as I believe is the case in Canada, or deductible only against imputed rent, as in Germany.

In this country, we do not charge imputed rent, but we allow full deduction of the interest. Today, the interest rate contains a large inflation premium, which is really amortization, i.e., reduction in the real volume of the debt. The government has made amortization deductible, in effect. No wonder then that people have found it smart to invest in homes.

We have done a number of other things, as you know, related to insurance, guarantees, and various government programs. We constructed a pipeline from the housing finance market into the bond market, through GNMA and other pass-through devices. All of these have been tremendous aids to housing. And what have we got? We have a set of results that in many ways is not what we anticipated.

We find that the nominal price of housing has gone sky high. I see in one of the papers that the real price of housing has come down—I do not quite know how to interpret it, but evidently the author did not just divide by the CPI. We have made the real return on homeownership very high. I saw one paper that said we made the marginal productivity of investment in housing zero. There evidently has been a tremendous shift from business financing to home financing. This has been accompanied by a shift in the ownership of wealth from the stockholder to the homeowner.

That means, putting it in its crudest form, redistribution from the producer to the consumer. Our productivity gains show that. We have gone from 3 percent as a general rule to 1 percent if we are lucky. At present of course we are seeing declines in productivity.

We have had other structural results from the strong subsidization of housing that we did not anticipate and may not like. There has been a severe drop in the saving ratio that I believe you discussed this morning, which may be related to profits on housing. There has been, as I said, a drop in investment relative to need, not necessarily relative to GNP and to productivity. There has been a reduction in mobility. If you think of the problem of somebody moving out to California, or even just moving within a state, it involves the sale and financing of a home which is difficult at this time. And we have been building the wrong kinds of homes.

At a time when we are down-sizing cars, we should also be down-sizing homes. But, the effort to invest as much as one can in a house, or more than one house, leads to an up-sizing that we cannot afford today. We have also created social tensions.

One wedge that we have driven is between owners of homes and new would-be buyers who have a hard time buying a home. We have driven a wedge between owners and renters. We have created a real financial elite—that is, the people who still have these 5 or 6 percent mortgages, who will not let go of them; even when they sell their homes, they find some wrap-around device so that the early mortgage remains intact.

It may be true that the homeowners are house poor, as they say; they have allocated too high a portion of their cash flow to their mortgage payment. However, taking into account their prospective income and prospective appreciation of the property—at least until now—they appear to know what they are doing.

On the cyclical side, as I said, we have also done a number of things to help housing. I think it is fair to say that housing was sacrificed a number of times to the needs of cyclical control. The way this worked is familiar: rising interest rates caused disintermediation; this disintermediation caused the crunch in the thrift industry and a downturn in housing. That made monetary policy effective, but in a very undesirable way.

We have protected the housing industry to some degree against that. First, there were much bigger flows from the Home Loan Bank Board into the mortgage market. Then in 1979 when things began to get a little difficult, the money market certificates which currently amount to nearly $300 billion were created. Other devices have included the 4-year note. Moreover, CDs are being insured. These are all devices to stem the financial pressure on thrift institutions, the area of the financial mechanism that generally finances housing.

These measures have worked for a while. But meanwhile, we have learned that they have their costs. First, by eliminating the availability of constraint, i.e., the crunch-type effect, interest rates must be relied upon to a greater degree. Therefore, interest rates have had to rise higher than they would have if the old mechanism of crunching the housing industry still had been in effect.

Second, it is not quite so obvious as it seemed a year ago or so, that protecting the housing industry against thrift disintermediation, and protecting the thrift institutions against this disintermediation, have done them all as much of a favor as originally intended. Previously, they had problems resulting from a loss of deposits. Now, their problems are more those of pressure on their surplus, pressure on their earnings. One way or another, it is very difficult to protect the thrift industry against the needs of monetary restraint. Hence, while a great deal has been done, the situation which emerged at the end is not necessarily better.

We have seen some additional complicated results of trying to protect thrift institutions against monetary restraint. They issue high interest paper, money market certificates, usually, and then they put the money into the federal funds market or some other high-yielding, short-term assets instead of into mortgages. Obviously, that does not help the housing industry very much.

It is problems of this kind that give one pause in thinking out what the best approach to this situation might be other than, of course, the obvious one that we ought to try to bring down inflation. I have said for many years that bringing down the inflation rate is an absolute must, even at Yale, 30 years ago. But, in those days, it was almost impossible to get anything but a laugh when we said inflation was bad. Inflation was considered probably good—it stimulated investments, stimulated employment, and who cared about the cost? There might be a little redistribution; some lost, others gained; but on balance it was a zero sum again. And, we went on like that for many years. That point of view was confirmed by the discovery of the Phillips curve, the most disastrous innovation in economics, I believe, that we have seen.

It is only quite recently that people are coming around to believe that inflation is bad. Now, I do not want to argue that case at all here. As I said before, productivity growth has slowed from 3 to 1 percent; I think inflation and the things inflation does are clearly associated with that. The ultimate cost of inflation is both a much lower level and growth path for GNP. I think that is as much of a case as needs to be made.

NOTES

NOTES TO CHAPTER 2

1. Inclusion of property tax payments in the cost of housing needs explanation. One may rightfully argue that property taxes are but payments for better community services (e.g., a better public school system), and for this reason should not be included as a cost of housing. This would be a valid criticism if our primary concern were with the choice of location of housing. Indeed, in areas where property taxes are higher, community services are better, other things being equal. On the other hand, our main concern is the cost of one more square foot of space when a house is being built (or remodeled). The additional property tax paid on this square foot is unlikely to render additional community services and thus is appropriately treated as a part of the user cost of housing.

2. For an analysis explaining relative changes in housing and rental prices, see Titman (1979).

3. These are survey data on expectations, but these data refer to expectations over short time horizons.

4. When taxes are considered, the nominal interest rate can rise by more or less than the increase in expected inflation. See Hendershott (1979).

5. A Box-Jenkins ARIMA process is sometimes employed to obtain estimates of an expectations formation process. This method is difficult to apply when the expectations are over multiple future periods.

6. The adjustment for energy and price controls are those of Gordon (1977) who kindly supplied the data through 1978. The rate of increase in the GNP consumption deflator, also stripped of food and energy, was employed for 1979.

7. The actual equation is

$$i_N = \underset{\text{(constr.)}}{0.024} + \underset{(0.02)}{0.99} \sum_{i=0}^{15} \phi_i y_{t-i} + \underset{(.014)}{.079} (CU - \overline{CU}),$$

where t ratios are in parentheses. The adjusted R^2 is 0.90 and the Durbin-Watson ratio is 0.65. The interest rate is significantly lower than predicted in the second, third, and fourth quarters of 1968, 1972, and 1976, all election years, and particularly high from the fourth quarter of 1969 to the fourth quarter of 1970 and the second to fourth quarters of 1974, both recession periods.

8. The difference was between 25 and 29 basis points throughout the 1974-1978 period with the exception of six months in later 1974 and early 1975 when the difference narrowed to 17 basis points. Because interest rates were exceptionally high in this period, the narrowing may be attributed to interest rate ceilings.

9. The interest rate premium (x) paid on the 15 percent marginal loan is 1.62 percentage points and is calculated by solving

$$0.75i + 0.15(i + x) = 0.9(i + 27).$$

10. The failure of interest rates to move with a multiple of expected inflation can be attributed to the use of historic-cost depreciation of capital, FIFO accounting for inventories and the taxation of nominal capital gains [Hendershott (1979)]. For an analysis emphasizing nontax factors that might account for interest rates not rising with a multiple of expected inflation, see Levi and Markin (1978).

11. Restrictions against VRMs have had a major redistributive effect in that they required binding deposit rate ceilings which caused a substantial income shift from lower income depositors to higher income mortgagors. For a discussion of the redistributional effects of deposit rate ceilings, see Hendershott and Villani (1977, chapter 6).

12. See Hendershott and Villani (1977, pp. 17-24) for a brief discussion of this argument. The most thorough treatment in this area is Modigliani and Lessard (1975).

13. See Villani (1978) and (1980), Diamond (1979), and Titman (1979).

171

14. For discussions of the distribution of the tax subsidy by income class, see Aaron (1972), Laidler (1969), and White and White (1977).

15. The real user cost for corporate plant is estimated to have been 25 percent in 1978 [Hendershott and Hu (1980b)].

16. Rosen (1979) estimates a productivity gain from eliminating the housing tax subsidy of $107 per family based upon his 1970 sample. Given that there were 40 million owner-occupied units in 1970, the total productivity gain would be roughly $4 1/4 billion ($107 times 40 million). Inflation and household formation since then suggest a gain in 1979 dollars of around 10 billion.

17. See Villani (1980) and Dougherty and Van Order (1979) on this point.

NOTES TO CHAPTER 4

1. As his subtitle suggests, Mayes's study, unlike earlier ones, does focus on "The Effects of Building Society Behavior on House Prices." Like previous work, however, the house prices considered are those of new houses. The choice of dependent variable is, as Mayes says, for "pragmatic purposes" (p. 48) and it is a satisfactory indicator of all house prices "... [if] movements in new and other prices follow the same course" (p. 51). (See footnote 2.)

2. Artis et al. use the Fair-Jaffee approach with the change in the real price of new houses as an indicator of excess demand in the housing market. They reject this specification, and this is not surprising when one considers more recent behavior of house prices: From 1974 to 1977 the real price of all dwellings sold (as measured by the Building Societies Association/Department of Environment sample) declines whereas the real price of new dwellings increased; by their approach this period would be defined as one of excess demand, a description that does not seem to fit the depressed nature of the construction industry (see Hillebrandt [1977]).

3. Keynes (1937).

4. See, for example, Byatt et al. (1973), Wilkinson (1973), and Rosen (1979).

5. There are, of course, other tax favored assets, particularly pension schemes.

6. See Feldstein and Eckstein (1970), Feldstein and Chamberlain (1973) and Fama (1975).

7. This does not imply that consumers are necessarily liquidity constrained, which would be incompatible with the permanent income hypothesis. It only entails that the additional borrowing they desire as a result of faster expected inflation may require tangible security. Taylor and Threadgold (1979) show the effect of capital gains on net monetary liabilities associated with inflation on comprehensive income of the personal sector and its savings.

8. Kearl and Mishkin (1977) have suggested that a higher anticipated rate of inflation may be associated with enhanced perceptions of uncertainty, which increase the demand for liquidity and reduce the demand for housing. Tobin (1961) has also suggested that a fall in bond supply (thus in real bond yields) may initially induce investors to rearrange their portfolios selling claims to real assets, including housing assets, thus tending to reduce their price. Saunders (1979) indeed finds such a positive relationship between real consol yields and share prices in the U.K. These disequilibrium influences of higher inflation therefore tend to operate in the opposite direction from the equilibrium influences.

9. Because consols have no maturity the observed interest rate is equal to the yield or internal rate of return. We utilize a six-quarter moving average of S in the estimation and lag it one quarter.

10. Note that the value of the tax relief on mortgage interest also increases with the marginal tax rate.

11. See Evidence by the Building Societies Association in [Wilson] Committee (1979) and [Wilson] Committee (1980), chapters 8 and 14.

12. From Hall's (1978) analysis, this should be a random walk with trend.

13. The instruments used were real value of gross domestic nondwelling fixed capital formation, real value of government expenditure, the current account trade balance, and the minimum lending rate all lagged for four periods and the predetermined variables in the regression.

14. Replacing HH with a seasonally adjusted measure of the number of marriages (as Hadjimatheou does) yields an equation with a Z (6) statistic of 13.9 and a Durbin-Watson statistic of 1.56. The standard error of the regression increases to 0.013 and, with M = marriages, the coefficient of $\ln M_{t-1}$ and change in $\ln M_t$ are not significantly different from zero; the t statistics for every other variable are also lower.

15. If these measurement errors are correlated with the regressors, then our estimates are inconsistent.

16. See Hughes (1979) and Atkinson and King (1980).

17. See Atkinson and King (1980) for some illustrative calculations.

18. See Feldstein (1976) and Boskin (1978).

19. See [Wilson] Committee (1980), chapters 8 and 14.

20. In a situation where the mortgage rate does not adjust quickly enough to clear the credit market there could still be credit rationing and a relationship between building society lending and house prices outside of equilibrium; see Fair and Jaffee (1972).

21. The opening up of competition among building societies provides a "one-off" upward push to house prices by attracting more funds into housing. This is probably offset by the effect of the other recommended changes on real house prices.

NOTES TO CHAPTER 6

1. The distinction between asset prices and construction costs is akin to Tobin's distinction between market value and replacement cost in discussions of business investment decision. Long-run equality between asset prices and construction costs is the same as Tobin's q = 1.

2. My data on household formation come from Census series P-20, number 327, August 1978. Data for starts come from the *Economic Report of the President*, 1980 and 1975. Starts data for the fifties is for total starts, public plus private. For the sixties and seventies, starts are limited to private starts. In view of their small number, the differential treatment of public starts should be inconsequential.

3. The copy of the paper I received contains no data appendix so I do not know where Hamilton and Cooke got their data. *The 1975 Economic Report of the President* shows 15,068,300 starts for the years 1950-1959 or 1.5 million starts a year. If one drops 1950, starts averaged 1.46 million over the remaining nine years. After reworking Census data, Maisel estimates that starts averaged 1.3686 million over the fifties. (See S. Maisel, "A Theory of Fluctuations in Residential Construction Starts," *American Economic Review*, June 1963, pp. 359-383.) All these estimates are substantially above the figures implicit in Hamilton and Cooke's figures II and III.

NOTES TO CHAPTER 8

1. See Friedan and Solomon (1977), Swan (1978), and Weicher (1979) for a discussion of "affordability."

2. This need not be true if rental and owner-occupied prices can differ. In the long run, this is unlikely and to the extent that condominium conversion is not inhibited, it will also hold in the short run.

3.   For example, FHA data are not representative and are not a properly drawn sample. FHA tends to concentrate on one type of house or location one month and another the next.

4.   For instance, the Commerce Department measure increased 163 percent from 1963 to 1978 while the CPI measure rose only 90 percent for the same base period.

5.   Recently, the Bureau of Labor Statistics published five experimental measures of the CPI. These included a rental equivalence and various user cost methods for measuring homeownership, the calculated weights for these alternative measures of homeownership were in the range of 10-15 percent for 1979.

NOTES TO CHAPTER 9

1.   U.S. Bureau of Labor Statistics [1981]. Prior to 1978 fewer areas were reported.

2.   Since 1978 the CPI has measured an average of rent changes over the last month and the last six months. See Thibodeau and Ozanne [1981] for discussion of CPI procedures and references to other sources.

3.   U.S. Bureau of Labor Statistics [1981].

4.   See for example Dougherty and Van Order [1981].

5.   Copies of AHS questionnaires are included in appendices to the printed reports of the survey findings. See, for example, AHS (1976), Appendix A.

6.   The research referred to in this section is fully documented in Thibodeau and Ozanne [1981].

7.   These indexes extend to the entire U.S., not just the metropolitan areas and urban places covered by the present CPI index.

8.   See Malpezzi, Ozanne, and Thibodeau [1980] for background on the equations discussed in this section. The equations were estimated as part of an evaluation of fair market rents in the Section 8 Housing Assistance Program. The rent indexes described are a sidelight from that study.

9.   The Saginaw AHS data tape was not released by Census because of confidentiality provisions.

10.   As of April 1980, 19 areas have surveys available for 1974 and 1977.

11.   The April 1974 to April 1977 CPI for all urban places reports contract rents rising 17.7 percent, fuel oil #2 rising 35.4 percent, electricity rising 29.0 percent, and natural gas rising 68.4 percent.

12.   The 12-month index without heat is $e^{12b} - 1$ and the corresponding index with heat is $e^{12(b+c)} - 1$.

NOTES TO CHAPTER 10

1.   See Gillingham (1972), Muth (1972), and BLS (1973, 1975, 1977).

2.   We do not agree with the conclusions reached by Hendershott and Hu in their paper in this volume that "Given the negligible cost of capital for high income households one should not be surprised to find high-income two-person families occupying five-bedroom, three-bath, two- family-room houses." Rather if the cost of owning such a house were very low for a high-income household, we would not be surprised to find them *owning* it. However, we might be surprised to find them *occupying* it, since their cost of occupying it is at least equal to the considerable foregone rent. (We are, of course, abstracting from the effects that mortgage restrictions and transactions costs have on a shelter consumption decision.)

3.   The difference between the average characteristics of rental units and owner-occupied units is often cited as the primary objection to the rental equivalence approach. However,

this should not present an insurmountable problem for our research, given the broad range of housing units represented in the CPI rent sample.

4. Perhaps 7 percent of the rent sample is subject to some form of rent control legislation. Given that the rental equivalence method attempts to measure the market rent obtainable for a typical owner-occupied unit, the presence of controls should create no particular distortions in the index. Of course, the possibility of nonprice rationing situations does present difficulties for the interpretation of either a rent or rental equivalence index.

5. The BLS has recently begun publishing several experimental homeownership cost indexes, including two user cost indexes.

NOTES TO CHAPTER 12

1. Jack M. Guttentag, "Selective Credit Controls on Residential Mortgage Credit," in Ira Kaminow and James M. O'Brien (eds.), *Studies in Selective Credit Policies* (Federal Reserve Bank of Philadelphia, 1975).